Silly Wom

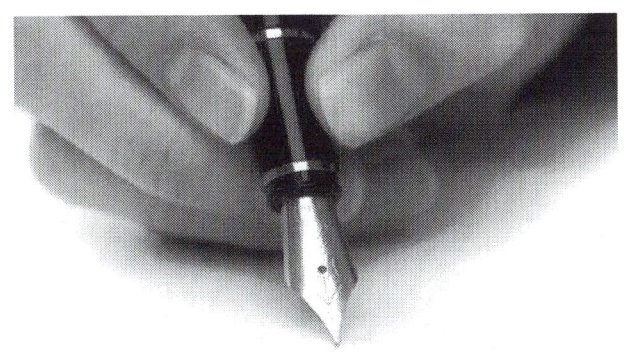

Green Pen

Productions

ISBN-13: 978-1461037941

ISBN-10: 1461037948

TO: Marcus
I'm Looking For your Play/Book
You can Do it   Be Blessed

2016

Silly Women

&

Sleepy Men

© 2012 Robert L Green
GreenPen Productions

All rights reserved. Reproduction, storage in a retrieval system or copying electronically or otherwise is forbidden without permission of the author, except for brief excerpts for purpose of book reviews.

DEDICATION

I would like to dedicate this book to my grandmothers, Cora Green and Marjorie Burks; my uncles, Darrel Burks and Walter Green; and a faithful member of my church, Shannon Davis, whom have all gone on to be with the Lord; leaving behind their imprint on my life, which has empowered me to fulfill my dreams.

To all of my family who loves me, supports me, and has taught me so much about life. The lessons and the instructions are priceless.

To all the brothers and sisters in the Gospel, who have ministered to me and have allowed me the honor and the privilege of ministering to them - I thank you. To everyone else God has used to touch my life, continue to pray for me as I pray for you.

And last but not least, I want to thank my church, Redemption Ministries, in Cedar Rapids, Iowa, for their support. God bless you all!

GREENNOTE

The relationship between man and woman has been discussed, dissected, and interpreted in every form of literature. Countless self-help and inspirational books have been written to help shed light on tumultuous, unexplored grounds for couples. Each person, is in search of the answer to what it takes to make their relationship a romantic, breathtaking, never-ending love story that is vital to their happiness. This narrative will show how we can be affected by bad philosophies, bad connections, and bad perceptions. The enemy of one's soul is very adamant about the things that can be distracting and cause one to self destruct.

Paraphrasing Job chapter 1 verses 6 – 12 in the Bible:

Satan says if I can get to the things that are dear to them, I'll make them self-destruct. The enemy knows every struggle; everything that you have not been healed from is like blood in the water. He'll come lurking around in the dark times in your life, waiting for the kill. He will consistently put you in overwhelming circumstances and seemingly force you to make decisions that feel and sound good at the time, but will lead to the destruction of your peace and total happiness.

Therefore submit to God. Resist the devil and he will flee from you. – James 4:7

Silly Women - 2 Timothy 3:1-6

Ladies, it is important to understand that the enemy wants to lead you away from the source of your power—the strength of your life—and to imprison you in a place where you feel as if you are drowning in a pool of all your bad decisions, with no means of escape. The enemy lures you away with things that look good; but at all times, the motive behind his actions is to lead you into captivity, to impose his will on your life by any means necessary.

Sleepy Men - Matthew 13:24-25

Men, God has entrusted us with our marriages, families, and finances. The more we understand this, the more alarmed and alert we must be when the enemy is on the prowl to move into our territory and set up shop. We must come back to a place of spiritual oneness with God so that we can see the enemy's works from afar, and get ourselves and our households away from the demonic fiends of the enemy that secretly take root and cause your life to explode. We must be careful of what is being implanted in our lives.

Chapter 1

In the beginning, it was just us…

On a warm summer morning in the Cayman Islands, sunlight tiptoes through the window across Alisha's face as she wakes up and looks at her left hand; *I wasn't dreaming,* she says to herself as she gazes at her 2 karat, emerald-cut diamond wedding ring. Alisha leans over and kisses her husband Darien on the neck.

"Baby, wake up. Our flight leaves at 12 o'clock," she said.

"What time is it?", Darien asked as he began to yawn and wake up.

"8 a.m.," Alisha answered. Darien turned over.

"You're my wife", he smiled.

"And you're my husband," Alisha replied. They began to kiss again, then she said, "baby this is nice, how can we afford a hotel like this?" Her question was interrupted by a knock at the door.

"Room service!"

Alisha looked at Darien and he looked at her.

"Aren't you going to get it?," Alisha asked.

"No, you get it," Darien answered.

Alisha sighed as she got up and playfully tossed the cover over Darien's head. She got up and grabbed her robe, fastening it tight and replied, "just a minute."

She opened the door to the hotel attendant, smiling from ear to ear and holding 12 red roses.

"Have a great day," the hotel attendant said, as he walked away. Alisha came back to the bedroom, giddy as a schoolgirl, where Darien was still lying in the bed.

"Baby, you shouldn't have!," she said. Alisha took the vase of roses and put them on the dresser. She returned to the bed, where Darien gazed into her eyes and said, "anything for my wife." Darien pulled Alisha in close to him, overwhelming her with deep, emotional kisses; and they began to make passionate love.

Afterwards, they got up and went downstairs to the hotel restaurant for breakfast, hand in hand. Darien pulled out his new bride's chair, she sat, and then he sat. The waitress came up and asked to take their order. As they began to place their order, Alisha gave Darien a strange look as he ordered eggs; Darien noticed, and said, "girl, what's wrong?"

She said nothing.

"Eggs are good, try them," he urged.

"I told you, I just hate eggs," Alisha said.

"Every time I eat them you seem disgusted," Darien replied.

"*No*, I just <u>don't</u> like them," she replied in an angered voice.

"Calm down, it's just eggs," Darien said. "We have been together five years now, and I have never known you to try them—that's why I asked. Sorry."

Silly Women & Sleepy Men

Alisha sat quietly for about two minutes as silence filled the table. Then Darien began to send replies to his morning e-mails, on his cell phone. He opened an e-mail and read it, and was ecstatic; he had been offered a promotion at the local Fire department. He told his wife the good news.

"That is great! You deserve it," she said. You have worked really hard for it."

Then Alisha got up. "Excuse me, I need to go to the restroom," she said.

"Okay," he replied. A few minutes later she returned to the table, about the same time as their breakfast arrived. The waitress handed Alisha her Belgian waffles, hash browns and bacon, and Darien his eggs, steak and hash browns. They bowed their heads to say grace. As they began eating Darien smirked, then laughed. Alisha gave him a weird look.

"What is wrong with you?," she asked.

"Did you see your mama do that two-step? I thought she was a Christian."

"Don't talk about my mama, when your cousins <u>clearly</u> had too much to drink before they came to the reception," Alisha cracked. "They celebrated more than we did—and we were the ones that got married! And then there's Anthony...how is he going to come to the reception, and not the wedding?"

"Anthony always has some weird story about what happened," Darien replied.

"And that's why I don't like him, because he's always getting into something. One of these days Anthony is going to get you into something you can't get out of."

"Yes, Mother," he said sarcastically.

Darien dug into his scrambled eggs and Alicia made that disgusted face again.

"Woman, do you see what time it is?," he said, looking at his watch. "We have to go. Our flight leaves at 12, and it is now a little after 10 a.m."

Darien signaled for the waitress and asked for the bill; he gave the waitress 30 dollars and he and Alisha walked off in a hurry.

Boarding the flight, Alisha looked at Darien and said, "I don't want to leave this place, it is too beautiful."

"We will be back if I get this position as Fire Chief," Darien said.

On the way back to Nashville, the newlyweds laughed about all the things that happened at the wedding. As they exited the airport, Alisha's phone rang; it was her childhood friend and business partner, Lindy.

"I hope you had fun," Lindy said sarcastically, because I had to hold down the salon by myself."

"How did we do this weekend,?" Alisha asked.

"We did alright," Lindy said.

Overhearing the conversation, Darien softly asked Alisha, "*how much did she steal from you?*"

Alisha looked at Darien, shaking her head, and mouthed, "*don't say that.*"

"Girl, I am going, though...we have to talk when you get settled," Lindy said.

"Okay," Alisha said, "I'll call you later."

On the car ride home, Alisha looked over to Darien and said, "I never imagined my life being so good. Here I am: 26, married, co-owner of a business, no kids, and on my way to finishing my degree program."

"Let's see if we can change that 'no kids' situation when we get home," Darien said.

"No, Mr. Energizer! I have tons of work to catch up on—and Lindy needs me," she said.

"You're not a miracle worker, Alisha."

"I know; but I have to be there for her," Alisha protested.

"You always *are* there for her, baby...sometimes you have to let experience teach people."

"It is no different from you and Anthony."

"Oh, there is a difference," Darien stated.

"Whatever," Alisha replied. "I still have to see about her, and you have to get ready for the next day."

"What about that situation?," Darien asked.

"What situation?" Alisha had a puzzled look on her face as they exited the car and walked up to the door of their house.

"The 'no kids' situation," he said, as they entered in. He began to hold her tightly, kissing her...and he was again interrupted by Alisha's phone; the caller ID showed Lindy's picture.

"Baby, I have to get this," Alisha said, going into the other room. "Baby? Don't forget my purse is in the car." Darien sighed, and went back to the car.

"Hello."

"Girl, you'll never guessed what happened to me," Lindy said. "Me and Will went to the club Saturday night, and he saw me flirting with some guys and started tripping!"

"Girl, I think he is crazy," Alisha said. "And how are you going to flirt with other guys, when you have someone with you already?," she scolded her friend.

"That guy was so fine; I had to get his phone number," Lindy said, totally ignoring Alisha's question.

"Girl, stop!"

"Here he is now on the other line—I'll call you back. Good bye," she said, rushing Alisha off the phone.

Alisha sat at the table doing school work, buried in books, and she began to drift off into sleep. Darien tapped her on the shoulder, waking her up.

"Come to bed, Alisha," he said gently.

"I have a little more work to do."

"You mean a little more snoring to do?," he chuckled.

"I don't snore," Alisha protested. "I'll be to bed in a minute."

As she started back to studying, Alisha fell asleep again. She began to dream of her childhood, right around the age of 11; she was in the kitchen with her mother, cooking breakfast. Just as suddenly, she was awakened out of her sleep again.

"Baby, come to bed," Darien repeated; this time, Alisha said "okay", and followed him to the bedroom.

The next morning, Darien got up out of the bed, awakening his wife with a soft kiss and a "honey, get up." He made a pot of coffee before proceeding out the door to work. As Darien got in the car his next door neighbor, Greg, stopped him.

"You're going to work so soon, honeymooner? I thought you would be working on your rug rats," Greg joked.

"I am," Darien chuckled back, "I have to pay the bills, too."

As Darien got in his car, Greg yelled out, "we are having meatloaf for dinner. You and Alisha should come over after work."

"If it is not too late and she isn't too busy, that sounds good," Darien replied.

On the way to work, Darien got a call from Anthony.

"Man, I am in trouble," Anthony said.

"What did you do?," Darien asked.

"I was about to buy a laptop from this guy," Anthony said, "and I thought it was cool; but I got into trouble with the law and I need to borrow $500 dollars from you."

"Alisha is going to kill me," Darien said.

"Are you the man of the house, or what?," Anthony questioned. "She won't know it's gone...I'll give it right back to you when I get out."

"Look, Anthony—I need it right back," Darien warned. "I'll send Tommy with the money."

"Are you talking about Tommy from high school?"

"Yes," Darien replied.

"Okay...hurry up!"

"Man, don't rush me!," said Darien, putting Anthony in check, "I'm getting right on it." He hung up and called Tommy, but got no answer.

Alisha got up, got ready for work, and left the house. She noticed that her driver's-side tire was a little flat and tried to call Darien on the phone, but his line was busy. With an appointment at the salon she didn't want to be late for, Alisha decided to just drive on to work. She put in her favorite gospel CD and turned it up. As she backed out of the driveway she saw Greg and waved at him, and then sped off. She attempted to call Darien again but the calendar on her cell phone beeped, reminding her of the time of her next appointment. When she returned to the call to Darien, all she got was the voicemail. Pulling up to the salon, she got out and checked the tire again and thought, *maybe it was just me,* because the tire seemed just fine. She walked into the salon and saw that her appointment was right on time.

"Good morning," Alisha said to her customer, "go ahead and sit in the chair, I am going to put some coffee on."

As she walked to the break room she heard her phone ring. *I'll get it later,* she thought. Alisha went back and started on her customer's hair. She had a good conversation going with her client, who asked about the honeymoon.

"Girl, it was awesome," Alisha exclaimed. "We went to the Cayman Islands, and we stayed in a luxurious suite. We went walking on the beach..."

"I am jealous! I wish my man was as good as yours. Girl, what is the secret??," the customer asked.

"You got to put it on him!"

Both women laughed, then Alisha said, "no, I am just playing. This is it, girl: you have to know exactly what to say at the *right* time and the *right* place," she explained. "Let me tell you what I do; I make my ideas *his* ideas, and I still get my way. Girl, I just take something he wants to do and just point it in my direction. For instance, when I wanted to have my honeymoon in the Islands, since the day he proposed to me I've initiated conversations about the beach; so on our honeymoon, *he* came up with the idea, 'let's go to the Cayman Islands'...girl, do you know what I said?"

"What?," the customer asked.

"CLOCKWORK".

The customer gave Alisha a puzzled look.

"What does that mean??," she asked.

"Every time my man comes up with an idea that I started, I smile and say..."

"...CLOCKWORK," they said in unison.

Alisha phone rang again, and she got it; it was Lindy. "Why didn't you answer the phone? I've been trying to call you."

"I was working; what is going on??"

"I thought we could hang out tonight," said Lindy.

"I'm not sure...I'll call you back a little later on."

"Girl, don't forget! We have so much to talk about."

###

Tommy waited on Anthony to be released from jail. Finally, Anthony walked out and greeted him.

"Man, I haven't seen you in years," Anthony said as they shook hands.

"Yes, it has been a minute," Tommy agreed.

"Man, let's go! I am so ready to leave here."

As soon as they got in the car, Anthony said, "man, I am hungry—you have to get me something to eat before you take me anywhere."

"I can take you home but I have some business to take care of..."

"...Man, I need a steak and I can't wait. Come on, man! I know you can spare at least an hour...so we can catch up on old times?"

Tommy sighed. "Okay, one hour."

"Cool! There goes one of my favorite restaurants, coming up on the left."

They pulled into the parking lot, parked, and proceeded to go in. They sat down at a table. The waitress said, "good afternoon, what can I get for you today?"

"Everything, baby—including you," Anthony flirted.

"I am *not* on the menu," the waitress replied evenly. She looked at Tommy, as if expecting a slick line from him, too.

"I would just like some water, please," he said. As they began to talk, Anthony started to tell Tommy some of the wild things he has been into over the past years. The waitress returned with Tommy's water and took their order. They ate, and then Tommy again told Anthony, "man, we have to go", as he waved for the waitress to come back to the table. "I have to go and take care of something," he repeated. Tommy gave the waitress his credit card and hurriedly took care of the bill. They exited the restaurant and got in the car, and he dropped Anthony off.

###

Darien got off work later that evening and called Anthony, but got no answer. *I knew this would happen,* he thought to himself. On the way home, Darien stopped at a station to get some gas. As he got out of the car and entered the station, he called Alisha.

"Hello, what's going on?"

"The neighbors want us over for dinner," Darien said. "Greg is cooking his world's famous meatloaf."

"Yeah...world famous," Alisha said sarcastically.

"What's all that noise in the background?"

"I am out with Lindy till you get home; I am getting ready to leave because this is a little too much for me—I can't wait to get home with you."

"Okay, I love you," Darien said, and they got off the phone. He headed home and got out of the car. He tried to call Anthony again, still no answer. Again, he told himself, *man, I knew that this would happen!* As he opened the door, his wife pulled up behind him in the driveway. Greg, who was looking out his window, came to his front door and said, "you are just in time for dinner!" Alisha saw Greg and said to herself, *God help me.* As she got out of her car she told Greg, "we'll be over in a minute." She went in the house and kissed Darien, saying, "hey, baby." He greeted her with no enthusiasm, and looked off.

"What's wrong?," Alisha asked.

"I really don't want to talk about it," Darien answered. "Let's just go over and have a plate of Greg's world famous meatloaf."

"Okay," Alisha exhaled, and put her things down as they walked out the door. They walked across the lawn to Greg's house and rang the doorbell. They went inside, greeting each other.

"Come on in, newlyweds. *Mi casa es su casa*" Greg said.

"What?," Alisha said.

"Just keep walking," Darien whispered. They made themselves comfortable and prepared for dinner. Greg and Darien had a conversation about the honeymoon and his job, allowing Alisha to just sit back, relax, and eat. After dinner, Alisha did make it a point to compliment Greg on his meatloaf. As they began their walk back home, Darien asked Alisha how was her day.

"It was the usual...how was yours?"

"I would rather not talk about it," Darien said. They entered the house.

"I have tons of studying to do," Alisha said.

"Why don't we watch a movie?," Darien suggested, " we never get a chance to watch movies anymore."

"Okay, maybe a little bit," Alisha said, "I really do have to get some studying done tonight."

Darien prepared Alisha favorite snack, brownies and popcorn. As the opening credits of the movie began, Alisha remembered that she'd left her phone in the car.

"You don't need your phone, you already know who is going to call you with her everyday problems," Darien said, not even trying to hide his annoyance.

Alisha insisted on going out to get her phone anyway; she got up, and Darien said "there goes the rest of our night." She went out to her car and got her phone, and noticed that she had 2 missed calls, one from a family member and the other one from an unfamiliar number. When she went back inside the house, Darien was no longer watching the movie and had gone into the bedroom. Darien called to her out of the bedroom.

"This time was strictly for me and you—not for me, you, and your phone."

"I'm going to put it on 'silent'—it isn't going to bother us anymore," she promised.

Darien came back into the living room, still a bit annoyed. He sat down.

"It isn't going to stop you from checking your phone," he said.

"Okay," she sighed, putting the phone aside. They began to watch TV and before long, they both began to fall asleep.

The home phone rang, and it was Lindy. Darien answered the phone.

"May I talk to Alisha?," Lindy asked.

He handed his wife the phone.

"What's up, girl?," Alisha asked, still a little groggy from waking up.

"I need you," Lindy said.

"But...it's 11:30p.m., and I am at home," Alisha protested.

"Girl, I really need you," Lindy said, sounding urgent. Alisha exhaled loudly. "Need me to do what?"

"I need you to come and get me."

"Okay, where is *your* car?"

"Girl...I am smashed. I can't drive."

Alisha was annoyed that her friend would impose on her like that; but she knew she'd go and pick her up anyway...after all, that's what friends were for...right?

"Where are you at?," Alisha asked.

"I'm at the club, girl," Lindy answered. "Just come and get me, it's only 15 minutes from your house...just come and get me."

"Okay," she said, resigned. Alisha got off the phone and looked at Darien.

"I already know," he said, turning over. His wife got up, put her clothes back on, and went out the door to go rescue her friend.

Alisha pulled into the club's parking lot. *I have to stop doing this! It has to end tonight*, she thought to herself. She called Lindy on her cell phone for her to come out, but she didn't answer. Impatient, she gave it a second try and there was a tap on the window. She looked up, and it was...him.

Alisha rolled down the window.

"Marcus! Is that you?"

"Alisha, I thought that was you," he smiled. "Girl, get out of that car and give me a hug!"

Caught by surprise, she got out the car and hugged him.

"I haven't seen you since high school," she said. "What's been going on with you?"

"After high school, I took over my father's business in real state. How has life been treating you?"

He held up her left hand with the wedding ring on it. "Oh, I see you're locked down," he said.

"I wouldn't call it that," Alisha said.

"Who did you marry?," he asked, prying. "I know you didn't marry who I think it is...I *know* you didn't marry Darien."

"Yes, I did" Alisha replied evenly.

"He is boring, and there isn't any way that he can satisfy a woman like you," Marcus stated.

"You're getting a little too personal." Alisha's voice was frosty. "I am doing just fine. Darien is a fireman, and I own my own beauty shop. We are doing *quite* well."

"I am sorry, beautiful. I just know that you missed your opportunity," he said.

"Opportunity for what?"

"Your opportunity to be with me," Marcus said, smugly. "Boy, _please_", Alisha huffed, rolling her eyes. "Anyway, it was nice seeing you."

"I bet," said Lindy who, by that time, was standing beside Alisha. They both got into the car.

"Oooh, I am telling!," Lindy teased, before moving on to her own story. "Girl, they were all over me tonight! You should come with me sometime...but it looks like you were getting some curb side service," she joked. "He was fine! Who is he?"

"No one—just someone from high school," Alisha said.

"I don't know about that," Lindy said doubtfully. "I thought I would need a crowbar to pull you two apart. I saw the way you two were looking at each other..."

"Believe me, girl—it was nothing," Alisha repeated.
As they exited the club parking lot, Alisha looked into her rear view mirror and thought silently, *the one that got away.* Lindy began telling her story about her night, but Alisha had tuned her completely out; she was rolling over in her mind, *what if?*

"Hey, you're going to miss my house!," Lindy said.

"Sorry, I'm just tired." Alisha pulled in the driveway and unlocked the doors so Lindy could get out.

"Thanks for picking me up," Lindy said.

"Okay...I got to get home, I am sleepy."

"You can stay with me tonight," Lindy said, "if you're sleepy, don't drive back home. All you got to do is get up early in the morning, then drive back home. Tell Darien you were too sleepy."

"No...he would fuss for days, and I don't want to hear his mouth," Alisha said. "I'm going to go—see you later."

"Okay," Lindy said as she walked to the door, and asked a second time, "are you sure?"

"Positive," she replied. Alisha made the drive back home. Meanwhile, Darien was calling Tommy. The phone just rang and rang; he got the voicemail for the third time. Darien left a message and hung up the phone. He noticed that Alisha still hadn't made it back yet, so he picked up the phone again and called her. She answered the phone and said, "baby, I already know."

"Girl...I don't like it when you're out late, and especially with Lindy; she is full of trouble."

"She needed me, and I had to be there—"

"—Stop!," Darien said, unwilling to listen anymore to his wife's excuses for her friend. "She was at the club drunk, as usual. I'm telling you, this girl is trouble! And furthermore, she needs some single friends to be with," he insisted. "You are a married woman, and your friends need to respect that."

"You're right," Alisha said. "Sorry, baby."

"Yeah, right...I'm sure," he answered blankly.

"I tell you what; when I get home I'm putting you to sleep, and you know what I mean," Alisha said seductively; she didn't want her husband upset with her.

"Mmm... how far away are you?," Darien asked anxiously.

Alisha purred, "I'm five minutes away, so get ready for me..." but then she yawned.

"This is not looking good for me; you are going to sleep, and you know it."

"I'm coming around the corner now," she said.

"Okay."

Moments later, she walked into the bedroom and took off her clothes. Darien looked at her and said, "Girl, I got a sweet tooth."

"What?," Alisha asked, with a puzzled look on her face.

"You know I need my brown sugar with me at all times, girl; come on and get in this bed!" She got into bed very seductively and kissed him, and said "Goodnight!"

"You played me," he said.

"Baby, I'm sleepy," she apologized, "tomorrow—I promise! I'm cooking your favorite dish, we are eating by candlelight, and I'll be wearing that new outfit you're always waiting for me to put on...so let's just go to bed tonight." She kissed him.

"...Just a little?," he asked.

"Tomorrow."

Darien gave in and called it a night; he rolled over and drifted off to sleep, but Alisha laid her head on the pillow and pulled the blanket up to her neck. She closed her eyes and reminisced about the hug from Marcus as she drifted off to sleep. Darien rolled over in the bed and placed his arm around Alisha, and she quickly escaped her "What If" fantasy.

Chapter 2

Do the right thing

The sunlight through the window awakened Darien, and the 7:00 a.m. buzzing of the alarm clock brought in the sound of Tuesday morning's normal routine. Darien got out of bed first and walked into the bathroom to prepare himself for a big meeting with the Fire Chief. He checked his phone; still, no calls...and he thought to himself, *I shouldn't have given Tommy that money.* Then Alisha walked in the bathroom.

"Is something wrong?," she asked.

"I don't want to talk about it," Darien answered.

Alisha kissed him on his back and wrapped her arm around him.

"I know what it is; last night, I told you I will make it up tonight—soon as we get home." She kissed him again. "Promise," she said.

"Okay,´ Darien replied. "Let's have pork chops and corn for dinner."

"That sound good," she said, "before I leave I'll see what's in the fridge."

"Okay baby, I'm gone," Darien said as he rushed out the door. Alisha tried to get a little studying in before her busy day at the salon. About an hour later, she rushed out the door and got into the car; she looked down at her phone and saw a text from Lindy: *thanks for last night.*

Alisha headed to work, and she called a few of her clients so she could schedule her day for some shopping later. While driving to the salon, she made a stop at the local coffee shop and grabbed a cappuccino and a blueberry muffin. As she went into her purse to pay the cashier, she was distracted by her cell phone as it rang repeatedly. She gave the cashier the money, and answered the phone.

"Hello, how is everything going?," the familiar voice said.

"Hello, Pastor Jones," Alisha said. "I'm fine, how are you, Pastor?"

"I'm blessed," he said, "how is that husband of yours doing?"

"You know him: work, work, work."

"We are having a prayer meeting tomorrow night for the community, and I would love to see you all there," Pastor Jones said.

"Pastor, I will try my best to make the prayer meeting," Alisha replied.

"Okay, I'll hold you to it," he said. "Hey, I know you're busy with school and everything, but I want to see you in church more—the kids at church miss you."

"I know; but I've just been so busy…"

"…You've got to make time for God," Pastor Jones urged. "I'll look for you all tomorrow night."

"Okay."

"Have a good day. 'Bye," Pastor Jones said.

"You too. Pray for me," Alisha said as she hung up the phone and pulled out her keys to go into the shop. As she entered the building, she got a text from Darien that said *I can't wait.*

Alisha replied to his text with *me neither! Now have a good day and think of me*, and then hit the 'send' button. Next, she called Lindy.

"Girl, when are you going to bring me my CD's? I need them for work," she said.

"You're up already?," said Lindy, "it's not even noon yet, and my head is pounding. I'll bring them, but for now you're going to have to sing yourself something—I've got to sleep last night off."

"Don't make me send someone over there to pound on your door, girl!," Alisha warned. "What happened to your job? Aren't you supposed to be at work?"

"No...I let it go. They wouldn't give me Saturday off, and you *know* I gotta be off to get my party on—and besides, they were tripping."

"You let that job go because you couldn't party on the weekends?!! You need help," Alisha said, "as a matter of fact, I'm giving Pastor Jones your number and telling him you have *plenty* of free time."

I haven't been to the church in a long time, have you?," Lindy asked.

"No, not like I want to," Alisha admitted. "We've been busy with school, and work, and planning the wedding and honeymoon, dealing with my outlaws—oops!!! I meant 'in-laws'...I've been going crazy."

Don't remind me—I was there! It was laugh-out-loud funny when your momma was on the dance floor, and Darien's cousins were all on me, talking about *'what's your name, girl?'* and I said, *'car note'*."

"You are crazy!," Alisha said. "Let me get off the phone, I think somebody is pulling in the driveway."

"No, I'll call you back," Lindy said.

"Okay." Alisha hung up the phone and opened the door.

"Hello, how are you?," she greeted the client.

"How are you? Girl, I love that shoe."

"Thanks, I got these at the mall at 40% off."

"I got to get some like that—they look hot, yet comfy."

"What's your name?," Alisha asked.

"Deana," the woman responded.

"Nice to meet you, Deana. Come on back, do you want to grab a magazine or something before we get started?"

"No, I'm fine," Deana said, "I just got this new touch screen phone and I'm still playing around with it."

"Okay, so what style are we going for today?"

"Can you show me some new styles in one of those books you have over there?," asked Deana. "I've got a hot date, and I want to look *good*—he might be 'the one'. He is an engineer; he's got everything a woman could want," she added.

"For real?," Alisha asked.

"Yes!," Deana said with certainty. "He looks so good, girl—he looks like a caramel candy bar wrapped in some "Lord Have Mercy!"

Alisha laughed out loud. Deana continued her story.

"He only has one child—and he's 18—so he won't get in the way tonight," she stated. "His son will be gone, so we can have some cuddle time."

"Don't hurt him," Alisha teased.

"I don't play," Deana said. "I'm 42 year old, and he is 34. He thinks he is going to do *his* thing, Hmm.. Momma is going to "Rock the baby to sleep", if you know what I mean."

Alisha was laughing to the point of tears, because after Deana said that, she got out of the chair and began to do a video girl dance.

"You are killing me, Deana!," Alisha said.

By that time, more clients had come in; Deana was entertaining everyone and the beauty shop was filled with laughter.

Meanwhile, Darien was at work and Tommy called.

"Sorry, man—I didn't have my phone, but I got the money...but he didn't send all of it, he sent $200," Tommy said.

"Classic Anthony," Darien said, shaking his head. "I knew it would be like this...but I'll deal with it."

"I'll bring it by later, 'cause I know you're at work and I'm on the way to work myself. Before I get off the phone, I saw your wife's friend in the club last night."

"Don't even tell me," Darien said disgustedly. "I already know! She called my house after 11 o 'clock and got my wife out of the bed to come and get her. And you know I was *beyond* mad, but that girl will do anything for

Lindy...I hate her! Lindy is going to be the end of our marriage."

"Man, you should tell your wife she needs a better class of friends—she's got too much going for herself to hang around with somebody who is not going anywhere in life," Tommy said.

"That is the truth," Darien agreed. "Man! Don't go MIA on me later, I need to get that money back in that account before Alisha checks it. I'll call you later."

Darien hung up the phone and went back to work.

Later that afternoon, Lindy was awakened by a knock at the door.

"Who is it?," she asked.

The voice on the other side said, "It's Will, let me in."

"You should have called first, what are you doing here?"

"Why are you acting like this? I just want to talk," said Will.

"We have nothing to talk about. We are through!"

"Open the door," Will demanded, as he began to rattle the doorknob very forcefully.

"Go away! This is a bad time," she said, then went into the kitchen, grabbed the telephone, and came back to the door.

"I'm calling the police, Will—just leave!," she shouted. Lindy was gently moved to the side of the door by her new late night fling: 6'3, 246-pound Tyland. With a towel wrapped around him, he said, "baby, I got this…"

"NO! Tyland…"

"I got this," he repeated.

At about that time, Will began to curse at Lindy as he walked back to his car; but Lindy was more concerned with trying to restrain Tyland. Finally, Will left.

"Thank the Lord," Lindy said, relieved. "Baby, I don't want you fighting someone who is nowhere *near* your size; and plus, what me and Will had is done, over!"

She kissed him, and said, "let's go back to bed, before you've got to go home to wifey."

"Don't kill the excitement by talking about her," Tyland said, "baby, let's focus on me loving you."

"You don't love me, you just want sex; don't start putting 'love' into it."

"Don't start tripping! You've got a random guy from the club you practically live at, so don't go there with me," Tyland said.

"You've got a wife!," Lindy said, raising her voice. "And what we are doing almost every night is *wrong*! And since we're putting it all out there, number one: I met you at that same club, so don't talk to me about how much *I'm* going out, because when you're not with me you are at home being 'the perfect husband' with your wife. I'm tired of you knocking on my door whenever you can squeeze me in, between your jobs and your wife."

"But still you call me, and we *both* knew all of that already."

"Number two: when we first got together, you said that you were leaving her," Lindy stressed.

There was dead silence.

"Oh! I get it; there's no need for you to leave now," she said.

Tyland has a confused look on his face. "What are you talking about?," he asked.

"If she gives you 80% of what you want and I give you the other 20%, *you're* the only one that walks away with the 100%."

"So now I'm using you, is that what you're saying?," Tyland asked angrily. "You quit your job, because you can't party on the weekend, and I still pay some of the bills in this house—and you're coming at *me* like I'm using *you*? Is all this coming from this guy at the door?"

"It's just the truth," Lindy stated, as she laid on the bed with her back towards Tyland. He hesitantly sat on the opposite side.

"Maybe I should go," he said quietly.

"Okay," she replied.

To make matters worse, Tyland's phone rang, and the sound of his wife's ringtone confirmed the unspoken thoughts that paraded round in Lindy's head. She gazed out the window as he answered the phone, "I will be there in about an hour; I still got a few stops to make." Then, accidentally, he hit the loudspeaker on his phone and the voice on the other end said, "baby I can't wait to make love to you tonight."

To Lindy, this was like a dagger to the heart; and she said to herself, *never again...I can't live my life like this.*
Tyland rushed anxiously to turn off the loud speaker, but it was too late. He looked into the bedroom and saw the look of disgust on Lindy's face, and he knew that this time was different. Lindy had heard Tyland talk to his wife before; but this time, something changed. It was a dawning of reality, the truth—and at any minute, the late night fling would be over. Tyland cleared his throat.

"I got to go," he said to Lindy.

"Okay. Let yourself out," she said.

As he turned and walked out, Lindy was left with a conflict in her emotions; she said to herself, *why do I feel this way? I knew what I was getting myself into...but why do I feel like this?*

She picked up her phone to call Alisha, but her line was busy so she called back; it was still busy, so she just laid in her bed, stared up at the ceiling, and put on some slow jazz music. Ten minutes after he left, Tyland sent Lindy a text that said *I'm sorry baby. I'll make it up to you,* but Lindy didn't reply. She laid her phone on the nightstand, and moped the rest of the day.

###

Meanwhile at the beauty shop, Alisha was finishing Deana's hair.

"I see you are married, how long?," Deana asked Alisha.

"Not long," she answered. "Are you married?"

"There's no way," Deana said, "there are too many young stallions running loose that need to be tamed." Alisha laughed.

"It's a dirty job, but somebody's got to do it," Deana added.

"Girl, you are crazy!," Alisha laughed.

"You're a good woman," Deana said to her, "you're willing to have the same thing over, and over, and over again...girl, how do you *do* it?"

"I love him," Alisha replied honestly.

"I love hamburgers, but I also love fries on the side, if you know what I mean."

"He's a good man," Alisha stated.

"Sometimes, you need Batman *and* Robin—that's all I'm saying."

The other people in the shop laughed at Deana's antics as she paid Alisha and started to walk out the door. She turned and said, "let me have a few of your cards, I have some friend at the office I'll send your way."

"Thanks, that would be great, because I need all the help I can get. I'm almost finished with school, and it's been a struggle."

"What is your major?," Deana asked.

"Business Management, and what do you do?" I'm the head of marketing at Berton Agencies."

I wish I had it like that, Alisha thought to herself.

"It will work out for you. I'm going to send some of my friends and co-workers 'cause they need you, *bad*".

Deana smiled and opened the door, and said "see you next time."

"Okay", Alisha smiled, as she watched Deana get into a beautiful black 550 Mercedes and drive off into traffic. Alisha went back to work and looked at her phone; she saw the missed calls from Lindy, but thought to herself, *I'll get with Lindy later tonight.* She began washing the next client's hair as her mind ran back to the arms of Marcus from the night before; and she thought to herself, *that's no place for a married woman, Wow!*

"Are you alright? You're not saying much," the client said.

"It's nothing, just daydreaming," Alisha said.

"You've got that look in your eye...what's his name?"

"Really, it's nothing...just thinking, what if things were different in my life. Have you ever wondered if you made the right decision?," Alisha asked. "Sometimes I feel as if I'm not sure; I love my husband, he does a lot of good things for me, and he loves me—I know that he would be any woman's dream. We are in love, but...sometimes I feel like I'm missing out on something."

"Well," the client asked thoughtfully, "is God in the center of your marriage?"

"Yes, but I haven't been to church in a while..."

"Baby, I'm not talking about a building, I'm talking about a relationship. Maybe what you've been missing is God. Without God, we can't do anything."

"That's true...I just want be sure," Alisha said.

"No, you are trying to weigh your options," the client said. "How long have you been married?"

Alisha hesitated, then slowly responded.

"A few days...but we've been together a little over two years," she said. "But here's the thing; before my husband, there was someone else. We didn't date, but he always flirted with me...and he would come into the store where I worked, and the scent of his cologne would fill the store, and every woman in there would say, 'who was that?' He always came in the store with his shirt open...you could see his dark chocolate muscles, and his clean-shaven bald head. In high school, his nickname was Sweet..."

"Well, why didn't you get with him?," the client asked.

"He was with somebody else at the time, and I didn't want to come in between them."

"So you're not a homewrecker, huh?"

"No!," Alisha replied sharply.

"Then why would you let someone break up *yours*?! As women, we have a built-in radar system that tells us when something is not right...and you *know* that this other man is not right. If he would flirt while he's with someone else, what makes you think that he would be faithful to you?"

"Yeah...I know," Alisha sighed. "When I saw him last night, all those feelings came back."

"They didn't come back, they never left," the client said, "you never closed the door on those feelings. When you are going into another place, you've got to close the door from where you came. Sometimes things from the past will hold us up from a better life ahead; don't let what you missed in the past stop your future, and don't feel like you missed out, because God knows what He is doing. Everything you need, God will supply. You've just got to be faithful to Him...and, you told God that you would forsake all others for your husband; long story short, are you familiar with playing cards?"

"Yes."

"Don't trade a king for jack," the client urged.

"I'm so rude...I didn't get your name," Alisha said.

"My name is Grace," she said.

"Thanks for that advice, Grace; you are very wise."

"Any time. I'm just a little old lady, trying to do the best I can," Grace smiled.

"Thank you again," Alisha said as she blow-dried the woman's hair, and they continued talking about life.

Alisha texted Darien and said *love you. hope your day is going well, I can't wait until tonight.* Soon after, she received a call on her cell phone.

"Hello."

"Hey! Girl, it's Deana, I'm working for you—I got a friend I'm talking to, they'll be giving me a call back later."

"Thank you," Alisha said.

"I got you, girl. We've got to look out for each other," she said. "We should hang out sometime."

"I would love to; whenever you have time, let me know," said Alisha.

"Okay, I'll call you back." Deana began to pack for a business trip to New York.

Alisha locked the shop door and started sweeping the floor, preparing to go home for the day; as Grace's words replayed in her mind, there was a knock at the door. She turned around and went to open the door for Lindy, and she walked into the shop.

"I tried to call you a million times, what happened?," Lindy demanded.

"I was *working*," Alisha said. "Oh! You're finally up, Sleeping Beauty!"

"I have had a Hell of a morning," Lindy said rolling her eyes.

"Stop cursing!"

"I'm not cursing. Hell is a destination if you don't live right, and I'm trying *not* to go...but these men are going to send me there."

"What's wrong with Will?," Alisha asked.

"He just doesn't do it for me," Lindy said simply. "Will's sex drive is in 'park', and mine is in 'overdrive'—plus, 'short-and-quick' is only good when you're at the doctor's office—*not* the bedroom...Will wants to change me, and control me...and then, on the other hand, there's Tyland..."

Alisha interrupted Lindy.

"Tyland? 'Married-with-kids' Tyland?"

"Alisha, *everyone* can't have the good life like you," Lindy said, glaring at Alisha.

"My life isn't perfect," Alisha replied, ignoring Lindy's dig, "but we just keep on striving."

Lindy resumed her storytelling.

"When it comes down to Tyland, OMG! This man needs to be on the cover of Playgirl," Lindy said. "Girl, when he comes over after his workout and his body is all sweaty, and his muscles are popping out all over his body...I stand in front of him after he showers and say "wow"; but one of the things that turns me on about him is that he is *aggressive*. I love that about Tyland, but I can't just keep playing as if he doesn't have a wife to go home to," Lindy continued. "This afternoon when I called you, he and I got into a big fight; then to top it all off, his phone rang and somehow it would *not* get off speaker phone, so I heard the whole 'I love you' speech...and he told me *weeks* ago that he was leaving—so, that what's going on in the wonderful world of Lindy."

"You've got to make some tough decisions," Alisha said, "but if I were you, Will would be my choice."

"Why?"

"He has potential—and he is the best person for you, and you know it!"

"Yeah, right!"

"I'm setting the security alarm; step outside, let me enter the code in the system," Alisha said ushering Lindy out the door. After setting the alarm, she walked with Lindy to their cars.

"I've got to be super woman tonight, thanks to you," Alisha said. "I've got to make up for last night."

Silly Women & Sleepy Men

"So, I guess I have to return those red 'hooker' boots I borrowed," Lindy chuckled.

"Yeah, right."

"You're still newlyweds, you shouldn't even *be* at work," Lindy declared. "I would be working on my headboard. You better start taking care of that man, before somebody else will! I'm your girl, and all I'm saying is if you start taking some time for him, things will start changing."

"He's good—I give him just enough."

"Okay," Lindy shrugged. "Don't call me when Darien is using his hose to put out somebody else's fire."

"Well, if he loves me he won't leave me," Alisha answered, defensively.

"You've still got to put some work in for him to stay! Look: all I'm saying is take care of your home—and I'll bring those red boots by later."

"Whatever," Alisha said, flatly. "I'll call you later, I've got some studying to do."

"Don't wake the neighbors," Lindy said, and they both drove away.

Driving home, Alisha stopped at the store to get her husband's favorite meal: baked fish, broccoli, baked potato, and cheesecake. As she raced home to put his favorite dish together, Darien was leaving work, headed home. He made a stop at Anthony's house, and he walked up to the door and rang the doorbell, Anthony came to the door and opened it with a surprised look on his face.

"Man...I was just getting ready to come and see you..."

"Yeah, right," Darien said, unconvinced. "You got that money you borrowed?"

"Look, something came up and...I only have $75—but I'll pay you off next week," Anthony said.

"Come on, man! I *told* you, I needed to get the money back. I'll be back you can bet on that," Darien stated angrily.

Frustrated, Darien got in his car and as he began to drive off, he saw a familiar face; he put the car in 'park' and got out.

"What's going on, Marcus? It's been a long time; it's good to see you, how has life been treating you?," Darien said.

"I'm good, man," Marcus replied.

"What are you doing now?," Darien asked.

"I'm in real estate," Marcus said. "My motto is if I get them in their dream house, they will keep me in mine. I can tell you're doing good, Mr. Firefighter."

"Yeah!," Anthony said, stepping out his door to join the conversation. "He is the big man in town."

As they stood outside Anthony's house, Alisha called Darien.

"Where are you?," she asked.

"Hey baby," he replied, "I had to make a stop—I'm wrapping it up right now."

"Where are you now?"

"At Anthony house."

"Okay honey, because I've got a surprise for you!"

Darien smiled. "I hope it's one of Victoria's red lace secrets, and those red boots I like that you gave away."

"No, you're so nasty...hurry home, I've got something you will like."

"Okay," Darien said, hanging up the phone.

"Anthony and Marcus, I got to go—I'll see you guys around." Darien left Anthony's house and as he was riding home, he stopped at the local floral shop to pick up some roses for Alisha.

It was 7:00p.m., and Alisha was preparing dinner. She pulled out her new scented candles, laid her lingerie across the bed, and put her radio on the jazz station. As she set the table and started to light the candles, she heard the sound of Darien's truck in the driveway. Alisha quickly lit the candles and came to the door to greet him with a kiss. Their neighbor Greg yelled across the lawn, smiling and waving.

"Hey! You two lovebirds get a room!"

"Let's take this inside, because I don't want the neighbors to call the police for assault on a fireman," Alisha teased, as she kissed him right across the threshold and through the door. Darien dropped his work bag and pulled her even closer. He began to kiss her more passionately, and started taking off her shirt.

"Whoa, cowboy! We will get there soon enough. I've got dinner for you, and it's your favorite," Alisha squealed.

"Yeah, it smells good in here," Darien confirmed. "What is that?"

"Those new candles I bought."

"I almost forgot—let me go back to the truck." Darien went to get the roses, and hid them behind his back; he walked back into the door.

"I've got something for you too," he smiled.

"Is it a size 7?"

As Darien walked slowly into the kitchen he answered, "no, it's 12." He pulled the dozen roses from behind his back as Alisha placed the baked fish on the counter and turned around. She smiled with pleasure.

"Honey! You are so...Mmm, I just can't put it into words!" She took the flowers and kissed him. "Let me put these in some water, and you go get cleaned up for dinner."

Just then, Alisha got a text message from Lindy.

"SUPERGIRL DO YOU NEED YOUR BOOTS"...LOL

Laughing to herself, she replied, *NO I can handle the man of steel LMBO!!!*

Darien came back into the dining room and sat at the table as Alisha began bringing out the food.

"Wow baby, that looks good—and I'm so hungry now," he said. As Darien told her about his day, Alisha sat down with him and ate dinner. After dinner, Alisha said, "baby, can you put the food away and put the dishes in the sink for me?"

"Sure, hun."

"Let me go slip into something more comfortable."

Darien finished and walked back to the bedroom. He opened the door, and Alisha stood there dressed in red. She came over and began to take off his shirt. They kissed, and he laid her down on the silk white sheets; the jazz took them into a romantic bliss as the candles' fragrance filled the room and moonlight shone through a break in the curtain...

Afterwards, lying in Darien's arms, Alisha looked into his eyes and said "I love you."

"I love you, too," Darien whispered. "Baby, I don't know where I would be without you. I know you never hear me say this but, you are a very strong Black woman. I look at all the things you do and I say to myself, you are a phenomenal woman. You are so smart, and beautiful," he said, kissing her.

"Aww, that was so sweet...but you are not getting any more. I got some studying to do, so...nice try, Casanova."

"Just a little bit?"

"You know I have a lot of studying to do," Alisha repeated. She went into the living room and laid on the couch; she opened her laptop and as she began to study, she drifted off to sleep. The next morning Darien woke and started the coffee pot. He looked at the clock and noticed that it was eight o'clock; he awakened Alisha who was still sleeping on the couch from the night before.

"I'm leaving baby, I'm already running late—I should've been at work at 7:30," he said.

Darien kissed Alisha and then walked out the door. Alisha got up off the couch and began to stretch. She looked at her phone and noticed a mysterious number. *I've never seen this number before*, Alisha thought, then she scrolled down her call log and saw that there had been no call from Lindy; *I'll call her later*. Alisha walked over to the coffee pot and poured some into her favorite pink coffee mug, then walked back to the couch and turned on the news. While watching the news, she received a call from Deana. Alisha answered the phone.

"How are you doing?," she asked Deana.

"Great!"

"How is New York?"

"It is great...last night was one of the wildest nights in my life—it seemed as if the night would never end."

"I wish it was me," Alisha sighed.

"No, you're a married woman, and some of the things we did last night were just crazy! I felt as if I was 21 again...we went to about three clubs, and you know what? I *had* to wear my little black dress..."

"...So you could show off your legs."

"Yes!," Deana replied, "and those young guys couldn't get enough."

Alisha started laughing, and then asked, "so what's on the agenda for today?"

"I have a few meetings to go to, then after that me and a few friends are going to a lounge," Deana said. "Girl, I know that you're married, but the next time I come to New York, you have to come with me."

"The way I feel, the very next time that you go *anywhere,* I'm going."

"I know you're stressed by school and working at the beauty shop...I tell you what—I'll bring you a little something back from my trip."

"You don't have to..."

"I know you're stressed, but there's nothing that a new purse and some new shoes can't fix."

"Come on, you don't have to do that!," Alisha protested.

"It's nothing for my new best friend," Deana said. "I have to run—I've got a few things to do before I enter this meeting, so when I get back to Nashville we have to hang out."

"That's fine!," Alisha said, "Just let me know when you get back, and we can hang out."

"Okay, I'll talk to you later."

Alisha got up from the couch and went into her bedroom and began to straighten up. She put on some uplifting music and started cleaning. When she finished, she tied her hair up and started running water for her shower. She got in the shower thinking of her husband, and of the things that happened the night before; then all of a sudden, the thought of Marcus flashed in her head.

"Oh my Lord, where did that thought come from?," Alisha said. She got out of the shower, got dressed, and walked out of the door. As she got into her car, she waved at the neighbor.

"Hi, Greg."

"Hi Alisha, did you hear what happened on the news this morning?"

"Yes I did," Alisha replied.

"That was some friends of mine," Greg said.

"I hate to hear that," Alisha said. "Well, I'll see you later."

"Okay have a good day."

Alisha got in the car and called Lindy back. As the phone was rang, she puts in her favorite CD.

"You will never guess what happened to me last night," Lindy said as soon as she answered the phone, "I met a young thang! Last night, he made me want to rob the cradle. Normally I wouldn't go under my age limit but, he made me want to do after school tutoring," Lindy joked. "Girl, you should've seen him trying to run all of that game on me! I told him, 'this ain't what you want'—I'll have you looking for me in the daytime with a flashlight."

Alisha laughed, and asked Lindy, "what happened to Tyland?"

"I'm not thinking about Tyland," Lindy answered. "He called me over and over again, but I didn't answer. I'm tired of that whole situation; it seems like the more we talk, the more I think about what happened."

"Well, I think you should wait until he straightens things out or makes up his mind what he wants to do, because I believe that he's a good match for you...but the fact of the matter is, he's still someone else's husband; and the more you ignore it the greater the problem will be," Alisha said. "But by the same token, you still have to do what's right. It's not even 12 o'clock—what are you doing up?," Alisha teased.

"I have to go to the doctor," Lindy replied.

"Girl, are you alright?"

"Yes."

"Have all of those one night stands caught up with you?," Alisha asked sarcastically.

"Girl, stop playing! I'm alright; it's just something weird going on in my body and I want to check it out. I'll be all right. I'll call you a little later on."

"Okay, talk to you later."

Right before Alisha started to drive down the street, she got a text message from Darien saying, *I love you.*
She texted back *I love you too.*

As she pulled up to the beauty shop and got out the car, she remembered that she'd left her coffee at home; so she hopped back into the car and drove to the coffee shop. Walking into the shop, she saw Pastor Jones sitting at a table and she walked over to him.

"Hey, Pastor Jones, how is it going?," she greeted him.

"Fine, how are things going with you and your husband?"

"Great."

"We missed you for the prayer meeting; I was really looking forward to seeing you," Pastor Jones said.

"I know, Pastor Jones. I just had so much to do; I promise I am going to start being more active in church...it's just that I have so much to do—between school and work, it seems like I have no time even for myself, let alone my husband, Pastor Jones...I've been really stressed out."

"Baby girl, you've *got* to make time for the most important things, and you've got to sacrifice for the things you need—and baby girl, you need God."

"Pastor, it's not just because I promised you I'd make time to do some of things I used to do at church—I miss being there. I really miss working with those kids."

"Well, start making time then, Alisha," Pastor Jones repeated. Alisha sighed, knowing that the only thing holding her back was herself.

"I've been a little stressed with some of the things that I've been going through with school and work and all of that, but I know God can see me through. I'm coming back to church; I've just gotta work this thing out on my own."

"Baby girl, if you could work it out on your own you wouldn't need Jesus, but the mere fact that we can't work it out on our own is an indication that we need Him—so whatever you're going through, make sure Jesus is in the middle," Pastor Jones said , taking a sip of his coffee.

"Pastor Jones, what type of coffee do you drink?," Alisha asked curiously .

"I don't get those new flavors, I'm old-school," he said. "I just like regular coffee."

"Me, I like hazelnut—it's my favorite," Alisha said. "How is First Lady Jones?"

"Fine! You should call her sometimes. She just recently went out-of-town to visit family; one of her family members got sick, and she went to pray for them and to visit."

"Pastor, can I ask you a personal question?"

"Sure, anything."

"What is the secret to being married that long? You all have been married for 38 years, and it seems like you guys are still happy after all of these years," Alisha said. "To be quite honest, it seems that you have just as much fun as most newlyweds and even young couples, from my viewpoint! How do you keep the fire and passion? How do you keep the drive to love the same person unconditionally all the time?"

"Baby girl, that's really simple; I used three things. Number one: I love the God in her, because marriage is a covenant *not* just with her but with God, and by it being a covenant, every time I want to be selfish and love myself, it's as if I'm not loving God and not upholding my covenant with Him; so I've learned how to cherish the God in her," he explained. "Number two: I love her unconditionally; through it all, my love for her will stand, and the only way it happens is I make up my mind that I will stick to my decision – to love for better or for worse. Number three, I openly talk to her about everything in my life—my life is an open book before her; there's no secrets or mysteries, and because of that she knows how to communicate with me—at the right times, at the right places—to be effective in everything she says and does. So, I guess number three, altogether, would be that you have to learn your mate."

"Pastor Jones...I still feel like there are some things that I just can't tell Darien. I don't know if he will be open to receive some of the things that I want to tell him," Alisha admitted. "I know honesty is the best policy, but I'm not sure if he can really handle some of the things from my past."

"I understand that—but Alisha, you *have* to have communication for your relationship to thrive and to work...and, baby girl, *silence* is the relationship-killer. Without a relationship, you have a marriage that is just an agreement; so, in order to have a really good marriage you first have to relate, and you can't relate without opening up."

"Pastor Jones, you are so wise! I'm so glad I have you my life."

"*I'm* so glad I'll see you at church Sunday."

"Pastor, I'm going to make it my business to be there—as a matter of fact, I promise you I'll be there."

"I'll hold you to it," Pastor Jones said.

"Okay Pastor, I've gotta get back to the shop, I think I've got clients waiting on me already—but I appreciate your time, and I thank you for everything you've done," Alisha said, hugging Pastor Jones.

As she walked out the door, Alisha ran into an old classmate April.

"How are you doing, Alisha? I haven't seen you in years! How've things been going with you?"

"Just great!"

"I've been doing fine too," April said, "what are you doing now?"

"I work at the salon," Alisha replied, "and I'm also finishing my degree."

"That's great, what salon do you work at?"

"The one downtown on Third Avenue."

"Okay...I didn't know you were there, too! I'm coming to see you sometime."

"Yeah, take one of my cards with you," Alisha said. "It was really good to see you April ."

Alisha got into her car and drove back to the beauty shop. She opened the door, turned on the music, then went back out to her car and got out a book to study before her first client showed up.

Darien was telling the guys at work some jokes he'd heard off an old television sitcom. He got up and left the kitchen area. Tommy came up behind him and started talking.

"I went to a meeting yesterday. I wanted you to go with me, but you didn't answer your phone," Tommy said. "Man, at this meeting they showed me how I can invest my money and get a return up to triple what I put in," he said.

"Tommy, man I am not getting into any get-rich-quick schemes," Darien said flatly. "I've had enough of them—all of them look good on screen, but actually trying them yourself? You'll just find yourself in a hole."

"Darien, I'm for real. I tried a little bit myself, and I do see some money coming back to me already. I'm telling you, this might be it! You need to come to one of the meetings with me."

No way," Darien stated flatly.

"Why not?" Look, these kinds of businesses have a trick: at first, you get a little bit of money, and then once you put in a lot you don't see anything after that."

Man, we're going to get *paid*," Tommy insisted. "Think about it, man—you can get Alisha that shop she always wanted, you can do some of the things she wants to do, and still work here...man, I'm trying to retire at 40! While you're here putting out bonfires I'll be on the beach, sipping on a pina colada, with a 20-year-old calling me 'Daddy'," Tommy laughed.

"No, you're going to be here wishing you hadn't done it, with nothing but lint in your pockets," Darien replied.

"Look: just let me go out to my car and get a brochure," Tommy said, walking out to his car. He returned quickly with a brochure and placed it on the table in front of Darien.

"Just check out some of the things in the brochure, and I'm telling you, it sells itself. Man, check it out, look at the website...man, this is a done deal."

"Okay, but I'm telling you brother, it's nothing but a gimmick," Darien said.

"Hey, did you get that money from Anthony?"

"Man, I really don't want to talk about it."

"I take that as a 'no'," Tommy said. He quickly changed the subject. "Hey, I found out about this new spot that's downtown, the new lounge opening up, man...we need to go check it out! I heard that there's nothing but women up in there. Look, man...I know you're married, but just come and hang out with me—and *I'll* hang out with all the women," Tommy joked.

"I don't know..."

"Come on, man—can you *please* put on the pants in the relationship and tell your wife that you're going out, and you'll be back later?"

"I don't know, man. I've got something that I've got to do at home."

Tommy exhaled, shaking his head. "Look, I know you all are newlyweds, but you don't really have to be with her every second of the day! We'll be in and out; I won't stay there long, I just want to check it out."

Darien thought about it for a minute.

"Okay," he said finally, "in and out, and after that I'm gone, Tommy."

"Cool."

As the day went on, Tommy told Darien more and more about this investment idea. Six o'clock came and Tommy got excited; but as they left the station, Darien has a bad feeling about going to the lounge. Tommy looked at Darien closely.

"I see you have that look in your eyes," Tommy said. "Don't worry, we'll be in and out."

"I'm good, man."

Later, while sitting at the bar, Tommy brought up the investment deal again.

"I don't know what excuse you have to come up with," Tommy said, "but the investment company is having a national meeting in Chicago in two weeks, so you have plenty of time to come up with a good enough excuse for Alisha to let you out of the house."

"Chicago? Man, I haven't been to Chicago in a long time!," Darien said. "I would love to go...as a matter of fact, I have family there that I haven't talked to in a long time. Man, that will be great, I wouldn't mind going out of town for a couple of days; how long is the trip?"

"It's for two days. They have seminars in the daytime, and in the evening, man, it's *really* great—they do everything first-class," Tommy explained. "Once you check the information out I have no doubt in my mind you're going to want to go to Chicago with me."

The waitress came over to the bar and asked, "Can I get you guys anything to drink?"

"Two beers—on his tab," Tommy said, nodding his head towards Darien.

"You mean *your* tab, right?," Darien said, looking at Tommy. Darien turned to the waitress and said, "it doesn't matter, one of us will take care of it."

Moments later, Tommy got a phone call from Anthony.

"Hello," he said, trying to be heard over the noise in the bar.

"Hey man, what's going on?"

"Nothing man, I'm downtown with Darien, what's going on with you?"

"Nothing," Anthony said. "Just looking for something to do tonight."

"Hey, come on down to the lounge and hang out with me and Darien."

"Sounds like a good idea—I'll see you guys in about 15 minutes."

Tommy told Darien more about the investment company and the trip to Chicago. He reached into his pocket and pulled out a brochure, then explained how the process worked and how fast he saw a return on his money. After Tommy explained it, Darien seemed more and more interested in the investment company. Anthony walked into the bar and looked around. He spotted Darien and Tommy and came up behind them, putting his hands on their shoulders.

"What's going on, guys?," he greeted them. Just then, the waitress walked up and asked, "what are you having?"

"A tall glass of you," Anthony replied eyeing the waitress up and down.

"Here we go again," Tommy groaned, hanging his head in embarrassment for his friend's lame pick up line.

"I'll have what these guys are having," Anthony said.

After the waitress walked off, Tommy looked at Anthony and shook his head. "Man, you have said that for years!," he said.

"Wouldn't it be funny if that line was to actually work one time?," Darien laughed.

"It has worked! Millions of times, fellas—millions of times," Anthony said smugly.

"Yeah right!," Tommy scoffed. Then Anthony said, "Say, what are these brochures out on the table for? I thought work was over."

"Man, we're getting ready to go to Chicago for a meeting—you wanna go with us?"

"You can count me in, I love Midwestern women," Anthony said, cutting his eye at Darien. "I know *one* person we can't count on—we already know that Alisha is not going to let Darien out of the house."

"Don't be mad at me if I'm trying to hold my thing together," Darien said.

"Darien we already know you're whipped," Anthony said. *Everybody* knows it. Just accept that you're whipped, you can't get out of the house...as a matter of fact," he said, turning and looking at Tommy, "I bet you $20 that he doesn't go. When is the trip?"

"In two weeks," Tommy replied.

Anthony said, "well, count me in with you all—I am going," and then he turned to Darien. "Man, we haven't gone out in a long time, especially an out-of-town trip. We need this, man—we don't hang out like we used to," he said. "I can't wait to go to Chicago."

"I really don't need to go out of town," Darien said, "I'm still recuperating from this honeymoon and the wedding."

"And speaking of your wedding, where is your cousin Frank?," Anthony asked, changing the subject. "Or better yet, Frank's sister? She gave me that eye."

"What 'eye'?," Darien asked, looking at Anthony questionably.

"Man, you know what eye I'm talking about! See, let me educate you fellas: when a woman makes a decision, she's not saying a word. By the time she does speak to you,

Silly Women & Sleepy Men

she's already mapped out the whole night. She knows exactly what to say to hold your attention, and she knows exactly what to say to make you leave her alone...I'm telling you, I got this 'woman' thing all figured out—if you just listen to me, you will learn something!"

Then, as Darien and Tommy laughed, Tommy said, "Oh! We're gonna learn something. Okay Love Doctor, let's see what you got."

"Man, it's very simple," Anthony said, as if he were explaining to small children, "you can tell by the way she says 'hello', you can tell by the way a woman greets you if she's interested in you. When you speak to a woman and she says 'hi...' ...real slow, that means she's interested—that she's really thinking about hooking up with you; but if she says 'hi' and moves along, that just means you've got 4 seconds to get her attention. You don't have all day, just 4 seconds—and if you can grab her attention in 4 seconds, man you can have her attention for a lifetime. "

He broke his theory down even further. "Now, women have *another* type of greeting: when they give you a lot of information up front. *This* type of woman I stay away from, because anytime a woman gives you a lot of information up front, it's always just the tip of the iceberg—and it's always going to be some weird situation that she's in."

"So," Darien said, a serious look on his face, "he has officially lost his mind."

Tommy and Darien burst out laughing, but Anthony was ready to defend his theory.

"No, I'm serious," he repeated, "you can tell by that 'hello'! You can tell by the way they greet you..."

"Okay Doctor Love, we get it now," Darien said. Darien got a text message on his phone. *Baby where are you? I've called you twice and you haven't answered the phone.*

Darien texted back, *I just went out with Tommy and Anthony for a few drinks.*

Darien, you know you shouldn't be drinking—that's why sometimes I hate it when you go out with them. They always influence you to do things that you know you shouldn't do.

Baby I'm all right, I got this.

You think...

When you talk to me like that, I can tell you think not, LOL.

Anthony looked at Darien and said, "it's written all over your face; Alisha is the only person that you talk to and makes you look like that! Man, you need to put your foot down...men wear the pants in the relationship, and the way I look at it, women need to be grateful," he continued. "If you really tell the truth, women outnumber men by a huge percentage—so they *really* need to be grateful. I had a woman that I was married to..." Anthony stopped in mid-sentence and said, "I just thought about it: 'me' and 'married' does not go into the same sentence...all I'm saying though, man, is you could leave her and find another one like her tonight. It's a shortage, and women need to recognize! Hey man, you know why women don't like me? Because I tell the truth, and I'm not compromising it, either—my way or the highway."

"Yeah...right," Tommy said, skeptically.

"I'm for real," Anthony stated.

Silly Women & Sleepy Men

Darien cut in, "I've got to go. I have things I have to do."

"Me too," Tommy added, "man, I have some things I gotta get ready for."

"The night is still young, why you guys going in so early?," Anthony protested.

"We have jobs, man...we have families," Tommy said.

"Both of you are whipped," Anthony said, dismissing them with a wave of his hand. Darien pulled out his credit card and said, "don't worry about it—it's on me."

The waitress came and took the credit card.

"Are you sure? I can get it," Tommy said.

"Just pick up the tab in Chicago," Darien said.

Tommy looked at Darien with excitement in his eyes. "So, you *are* going?"

"Let's just say the Windy City is going to get a taste of us country boys," Darien said.

Tommy shook his hand and said, "I can't wait, it's going to be like old times."

As they walked out and got into their cars, Anthony walked up behind them, a smug look on his face, and said "I told you it works—I got that waitress' phone number."

"I can't believe those old lines work," Darien said.

"KFC will run out of chicken before I run out of lines," Anthony said. "You haven't seen anything yet until we go to Chicago—I'm pulling out my 'A' material."

Darien laughed and said, "I'm out—talk with you guys later, I've got to go." He hopped into his truck and drove off.

As he headed home, Darien thought to himself, *this could be a great opportunity to make some extra money—and I can finally get into the real estate game, if I can get some extra money...God, please let this work out—because I can't afford to lose any more money...*

Darien got another text message from Alisha.; it said, *where are you? what's taking so long!* He looked at the text message then thought, *I'll just deal with it when I get home.*

Moments later, Darien pulled into the driveway. He put the truck into 'park'; *I really don't feel like dealing with this today,* he said to himself. He held his head down for a minute, just gathering his thoughts. He received another text message, this time from Tommy, saying *don't back out now man, we're counting on you.*

Darien answered, *we'll work it out, don't worry about it.*

Alisha looked out the window and wondered what was taking Darien so long to get out of the truck. He looked like he was out there in deep thought. Then Darien opened the door and got out. As usual, Greg the neighbor walked across the grass and started a conversation with him.

"How was work?," Greg asked.

"It was okay," Darien responded, distracted.

"Are you alright, neighbor? You seem to be troubled; what's really going on?"

"I just have to make some decisions on some things that I'm really not clear about," Darien explained. "Have you heard about this new investment company that has just moved into town?"

"A friend of mine was telling me about something of that sort last week. I told him, I don't have any more money to tie up into any pipe dreams because man, the only people who really see money in those types of organizations are the people on top!," Greg said. "Man, we *never* see any money. I've even tried some of the ones on TV, and it just doesn't work out. The money that you spend investing in those companies, you can just save that money and live off that."

"Well, that makes sense...I just want to make sure I'm doing the right thing. I have a friend who really wants me to go with him to one of these big informational meetings, but I don't know if I'm going because all of that sounds good when they're standing and explaining it; but when you're frustrated because you have their product and nothing seems to be working as it was advertised, you're stuck. You put all that time and effort in for nothing."

"Well," Greg said, thoughtfully, "the best thing to do is research the company and try to find some real testimonials of people that you can probably contact, or somebody that you know."

"Definitely! I'm probably going to check it out tonight."

"Where's the big meeting going to be?"

"In Chicago," Darien said.

"Chi town, the Windy City...I got in a lot of trouble back in my days in Chicago," Greg reminisced.

"Well...I'll be seeing you, let me go on to the house."

"Hey, I have my world-famous spaghetti tonight. You and 'Honey Bun' can come on over."

"I've got to raincheck your invitation; there are a few things we have to do tonight, but thanks, Greg."

"Oh, it's okay—but you're missing out."

Darien walked into the house, "honey I'm home."

"What took you so long?," Alisha asked, walking down the hallway.

"I was out with the guys, and we stopped at a lounge downtown."

"Darien, you already know how I feel about that! You drink beer every time you get around them, it's always something."

"What do you mean? I only had two beers."

"Still, you already know how I feel about it—I don't like it, I hate it. You promised me that you wouldn't do it."

"Why do you have all of this attitude over two beers? I'm not drunk. All I had was just two beers, and now I have to deal with all of this—*added* to the two beers! Give me a break."

"Give me a break, are you serious? When you clearly disrespect me by doing something like this? Darien, I *don't* want you to drink!"

"Okay, okay," Darien grumbled.

"I hate it when you're with them—every time you're with them, you're always liable to do something stupid," Alisha said angrily.

"Baby," Darien said cautiously, taking a step towards her, but Alisha put her hand in his face dismissively, then walked off down the hallway.

Darien turned around and went to the kitchen table and took a seat. He hollered down the hallway, "what's for dinner?"

"Beer!," Alisha replied.

Darien got up from the table and went to look in the refrigerator. Alisha came back into the kitchen.

"Just sit down, I've got this," she said.

"If you're going to do it with an attitude, don't do it at all," Darien said. Alisha looked at Darien.

"Move, Darien—I told you, I've got it."

Darien went and sat at the table.

"What's with you?," Alisha asked Darien, "I saw you outside sitting in the truck with your head down...what are you so deep in thought about?"

"It's nothing," Darien said, as Alisha went about preparing dinner. "Well...how would you feel if I told you there was an opportunity to make more money?," he asked.

"What type of opportunity?"

"Well, Tommy was telling me about an investment company that is new to the area, and he said that it works really well. He said within a few months you will see a return on your investment."

"No way!," Alisha said quickly. "Darien, don't you go out here and spend our money on some fly-by-night company."

"Girl, I haven't said that this was something I was going to do, it was just something I was thinking about...Alisha, we really do need the money. Think about it—there would be more money coming into the house, we'd get a chance to do some of the things that we want to do..."

"No! No way, Darien. I don't have a good feeling about this. Besides, where are we going to get the money? I already know what we spent on the wedding, and plus what we spent on this ring; and not to mention the honeymoon. Baby, we just don't have it like that."

"Think about it, this might be an opportunity to do some of the things that I want to do," Darien said.

"Oh, so it's all about what *you* want to do?"

"It's not about everything I want to do, I compromise all the time!," Darien came back at her. "Who do you think is paying for your schooling? Who do you think pays the majority of the bills that come into this house? This *could* be a great opportunity for us to get ahead."

"Oh, so *now* you're talking to me as if I don't do anything in this house; as if *I* don't pay any bills in the house, so *you* have the right to make all of the decisions! Darien, we are married. I am entitled to have just as much say-so as you do—regardless of what I bring to the table! Just because you make all the money doesn't give you the right to trample all over me."

Darien shook his head, trying to control his growing frustration. "This is classic, Alisha—you make everything all about you, and you miss the purpose and the point of what I'm trying to tell you!"

"No I don't—I just don't agree with everything you're saying. I'm not making it all about me, I'm looking out for the best interest of the entire household. I don't have a good feeling about this, and I don't like it."

"Right, I'm sure. You know what? Just drop it. Just forget I even said anything about it."

Darien sat at the table and ate his dinner in silence. Alisha walked away, whispering, "Lord help me, give me strength!"

She walked down the hallway back to the bedroom and promptly got on the phone to call Lindy.

"What's going on, girl?," Lindy greeted Alisha.

"Nothing, just Darien *tripping*, and out of his mind," Alisha said, sighing.

"I know what you need to do: get out of the house and come go out with me tonight. I promise I won't take you anywhere crazy, and I'll have you in at a decent time."

"Yeah, that would be nice, but...I don't know. I still have a lot of studying to do."

"Come on, it will be a lot of fun!," Lindy coaxed. "And you probably *need* to get out anyway."

"I don't know..."

"...yes you do!," Lindy stated with certainty. "You want to do this. I'm getting dressed, you're getting dressed, you're going to meet me at my house in an hour, we're gonna go out and have a few drinks, we'll have a little fun, then you're going home—that's it! Don't trip. I'm getting dressed now..."

"Well..." Alisha hedged, but Lindy wasn't taking 'no' for an answer.

"Look, Alisha! We need this. We need to get out."

"Alright. Maybe for an hour or so, but I've really got to get back home and study," she said. "You *know* I really don't go out on weekdays."

"I know—I gotcha, college girl."

"I'm not going to let you go out while I stay at home and catch it," Alisha said. "I'll call you in a little while when I'm on my way."

"Okay," Lindy said, hanging up the phone. She called Alisha back moments later and said, "bring those golden earrings."

"Okay," Alisha laughed and hung up the phone.

Darien was in the living room, watching the news on TV. He hollered back to the bedroom to Alisha and said, "baby, you want to watch a movie?", but there was no response from Alisha. *Oh, she must be asleep*, he thought. He sat on the couch with the brochures from Tommy in his hand as he looked over the information on the investment company and watched the news. About 30 minutes later, Darien heard the shower running. He got up from the couch and went back into the bedroom. Opening the door, he noticed that clothes were laid out on the bed. He went into the bathroom.

"I didn't know you were going somewhere; were you even going to tell me?," he asked his wife.

"Yes, I was going to tell you, Darien."

"I thought you had so much studying?"

Alisha exhaled loudly. "I just need to go out and clear my head," she said. "I'm just really stressed out about all of the work and studying, sunup to sundown. Darien, I thought you would understand that—you should know how stressed out I am."

"Once again, this is turned around on *me*: on what I *'should'* know and what I *'should'* do." Darien turned away and said, "well I'm going back to watch TV." Realization hit Darien and he stopped in his tracks, turning back around.

"You must be going with Lindy."
As expected, Alisha answered yes.

"I think that you need stop hanging out with Lindy. She is bad news, and everybody knows it," Darien warned.

"I'm not getting into any trouble, baby—pass me the towel," Alisha said casually, as she stepped out of the shower.

Darien walked back into the bathroom with the towel; he stopped for a minute and looked at Alisha.

"I know that you're in a hurry, young lady, but you got to pay the toll to get across this bridge," he said playfully as he began to take off his shirt.

"Oh no, put it back on," Alisha said, "I don't have time, and after your start in the kitchen, the candy shop is closed." She walked up to Darien, took the towel, and strolled right past him. Darien grabbed at the towel.

"Stop, Darien! You are so nasty!," she said. As Alisha got dressed, Darien went back into the living room and began to watch TV again. Alisha put on her black top, black skinny jeans, and black, 6-inch Nine West high-heeled shoes. Once Alisha finished dressing, she went out and got a drink of water, got her keys off the counter, and walked by Darien in the living room. Darien looked her over from head to toe.

"Where do you think you're going like this? You can't go out like that!," he said. "You never go out with *me* like that."

"What are you talking about?," Alisha asked. "Yes I do, I go out with you all the time like this."

"No! You don't go out with me like that."

"Yes, I do. Baby, I do not know what you're thinking, but I'm not going to stay out real late—I'm just gonna go out for awhile with Lindy, have a little fun, and come home."

"Alisha, come home at a decent time; you're not single anymore, you're married."

"I know—and I'm *not* going to stay out all night." She came over to Darien on the couch and kissed him. "I promise," she said.

"Okay," Darien pouted.

"I promise," Alisha repeated, kissing him again.

"Who are you smelling all good for?," Darien asked playfully.

"Nobody—just you." She kissed him and said, "I tell you what: when I come back, we're going to do that little thing we did when we first met."

Darien cracked a smile. "You need to hurry up and come back," he said.

Alisha walked out the door and got into the car. Shortly after she'd picked up Lindy, she received a phone call from Deana.

"Hey girl, what's going on?"

"Nothing much; I'm going out with a friend of mine," Alisha replied.

"Hey, you all should come to this party that a friend of mine is having—there's going to be plenty of food, drinks, and the 'who's-who' of the city."

"Hold on a minute," Alisha said. She turned the radio down and said to Lindy, "hey, let's check out this party that a friend of mine wants us to go to."

"Are you talking about the party that's going on in the hills?," Lindy asked excitedly. Alisha got back on the phone with Deana.

"Is it the party that's in the hills?," she asked.

Yes," Deana answered.

"We'll be there!," Lindy shouted in the background.

"Deana, give me the address so I can put it in my GPS," Alisha said. Deana gave her the address, then Alisha told her that she'd call when she was outside to let Deana know they'd arrived.

"Okay, talk to you later," Deana said. Alisha hung up the phone and looked at Lindy.

"I know what you're thinking, but I'm *still* not staying out late," Alisha said.

"Come on, girl! You've got to bend the rules tonight, this is a big party...everybody who's anybody is going to be there! So can you *please* <u>not</u> be a party pooper tonight?," Lindy urged. "I know what: as soon as we get there, I'm getting you some drinks to loosen you up."

"No, you're not!," Alisha insisted. "If I go home smelling like alcohol, Darien is going to hit the ceiling."

"Oh! That's my song on the radio," Lindy said, ignoring Alisha's protests. "Turn that up!"

Moments later as they arrived at the address in the hills, Lindy said, "this must be the place, look at all of these expensive cars...I told you there's nothing but ballers here. Let me fix my makeup!"

Alisha put the car in 'park' and sent a text message to Deana saying, *I'm here.*

She took one last look at herself in the mirror, and she and Lindy got out of the car and walked up towards the house. As Alisha approached the party, seeing all the people outside and hearing the music from a half a block away, she thought to herself, *I know this night is not going to go well for me.* Lindy looked over at Alisha.

"I see that look in your eyes," Lindy said. "Don't start tripping!"

Walking up the driveway, Alisha felt guilty so she took out her phone and sent Darien a text message saying, *I love you. I will see you soon.*

As they approached the door Deana came out, saying, "hey, girl!" and hugged Alisha.

"Let me introduce you to my friend," Alisha said, "this is Lindy." Lindy shook Deana's hand.

"How's it going?," Deana asked pleasantly.

"Good! Nice to meet you," Lindy said, and they all walked into the party. Deana took them around and introduced them to the people at the party. As Alisha was being introduced, she felt a little bit uncomfortable by the way that Deana was holding her hand. Alisha reasoned within herself, and said *maybe this is just how she is; it's harmless.*

As they walked through the party, Lindy started to feel left out; she wandered off from Alisha and Deana, and began to mingle with other people there. Deana led Alisha to a place to sit, then asked what she wanted to drink.

"Do you want something? They have shrimp and chicken, and some other stuff," Deana offered.

"I can get it myself," Alisha said.

"No problem, I was going up there anyway."

"In that case, a little shrimp will be fine."

As Deana walked off, Lindy came up to Alisha.

"Why are you sitting over here all by yourself with her?," Lindy questioned. "Get up and mingle—well, at *least* get up and dance."

"Deana's getting me something to eat."

"Okay," Lindy said, "go get yourself something from the bar."

"Deana is bringing me something to drink, too," Alisha said. Lindy raised her eyebrows.

"Oh! So you are Queen Elizabeth now; you got servants, Alisha? Why are you acting all brand-new in front of this lady?"

"What are you talking about?"

"You're tripping," Lindy said, shaking her head.

When Deana walked back over with the food and a drink for Alisha, Lindy walked off. Deana gave Alisha the plate and drink.

"I didn't want anything alcoholic to drink," Alisha said.

"A little bit won't hurt, we're celebrating."

"Celebrating what?"

"Being free," Deana said.

"I'm not free—I'm serving a life sentence," Alisha said, and showed off her ring. "What happened to the man you were telling me about at the shop a couple of days ago?"

"I had to let him go; he was trying to control, baby! A man that makes less money than me can never tell me what to do," Deana declared. "I do what I want to do—nobody controls, that's why my first marriage didn't work, because 'compromise' was a cuss word in my house—so that's why I'm single and free to mingle."

"I remember my days of being free; but I have a good man, so it's okay."

"That's good; but as for *me*, I love my freedom too much to sign up for jail, so I won't be able to do the 'married' thing again," Deana said. "Why are you babysitting this drink? Have some fun!"

Alisha hesitated, and then took a sip.

"Girl, your husband won't even let you drink... Bondage!," Deana mocked. "Have a little fun, Church Girl!"

Lindy watched from across the room, and she thought to herself, *I thought I was a bad influence!* Lindy started to make her way back over to Alisha's seat, but as she began moving through the crowded room, she found herself face-to-face with a guy who had been trying to make eye contact with her all night. He leaned over and whispered in her ear.

"I've been watching you all night, and I can't take my eyes off you...what's your name?," he asked.

"My name is Angel," Lindy told him.

"I see; I didn't know heaven could fit in that dress," he said approvingly. "My name is MJ."

"Don't you own a restaurant on the south side of town?," Lindy asked; she'd heard that name before.

"Yes, that's my family's restaurant...can I buy you a drink?"

"Yes, maybe later—I've got to get back to my girls," Lindy said.

"They are grown, and can make it on their own," MJ countered.

"Well...I do have to get back to them, but I will catch up with you later."

"Alright, Angel. I'm looking forward to that conversation with you."

Lindy walked over to Alisha and joined the conversation with Deana about marriage.

"I see that ring on your finger; are you in bondage, too?," Deana asked Lindy.

"No this is my mother's wedding ring. She died two years ago."

"I'm sorry."

"That's alright, girl! I'm free," Lindy said. They all laughed, and Deana high-fived Lindy. As the night went on, they talked more and more about men. Alisha looked at her watch.

"We've got to go. It's 12:30am, and I have to drive all the way to the other side of town," she said, obviously anxious.

"Okay," Lindy said.

"We were just having fun, can't you stay a little while longer?," Deana asked. "I hate to see you go—you all are so much fun."

"It's already late, and I really have to go—I have some things I have to do in the morning, and plus my husband is going to kill me when I get home," Alisha said.

"I have one meeting in the morning; maybe we can get together for brunch?," Deana suggested.

"Sounds good, just call me."

"That's too early for me," Lindy said. "I guess I'll see you when I see you; it was nice meeting you."

"Likewise—now go ahead and get the jailbird back to the warden," Deana joked.

"Yes I don't want my honey to send the FBI after me, so just give me a call tomorrow," Alisha said.

"Okay, I'll walk you guys out," Deana said. Lindy found a pen and wrote her number on a magazine page, tore it out, and folded it up. As she passed MJ in a crowd of people, he turned to her and she put the folded piece of paper in his pocket.

"Call me," Lindy said.

"You're leaving?"

"Yes, I gotta go."

MJ reached into his pocket opened up the folded page.

"Okay...I'll call you soon as I leave here," he smiled. Lindy waved as she walked off.

"I'll watch you until you get to your car," Deana said as Alisha and Lindy walked out the door.

"Okay," Alisha said, waving.

"Again, It was nice meeting you, maybe we can hang out another time," Lindy said.

"Call me when you get home," Deana said to Alisha, "just let me know that you made it safely."

"Okay," Alisha replied; as they walked down the driveway, Alisha looked back at Deana and noticed that she had a weird look on her face. When Alisha got back to her car, she noticed that Darien had only called once.

"I know he's called about a million times," Lindy said.

"No, just once...that's the strange thing."

"You want me to go home with you? I'm scared for you... maybe he's hiding behind the door and as soon as you walk in, he's going to make you *'eat the cake, Anna May!'*," Lindy joked, using her best Ike Turner voice from "What's Love Got To Do With It?"

They both started laughing. As they prepared to go, Lindy noticed Alisha fidgeting with the keys.

"Girl, you okay?," she asked. "Do you need me to drive? You *have* been drinking."

"No, I got it; I'm fine," Alisha said.

"Are you sure? I can take the wheel if needed."

"No, I *got* it," Alisha repeated.

"Okay! One swerve, and you're pulling over," Lindy warned. Lindy pulled out her phone, and noticed that she had 4 missed calls from Tyland. "It must be that time," she mumbled to herself.

"Don't say anything about what time it is...don't remind me," Alisha said.

"No, I wasn't talking to you—I'm talking about Tyland."

"I thought you were talking about letting him go?"

"I did; but, of course, he's still trying to get back with me," Lindy explained. "You wouldn't believe it, but the other night he came back to my house, unannounced! And you *well* know that in my book, *that* is a no-no. Girl...I really don't know what to do about Tyland."

"You know what to do—leave him alone! After all, he's still with his wife; obviously he has made up his mind about you."

"I know, but it's hard for me to let him go, considering all of the time we spent together...we have been together for some time now, and it's just so hard for me to let him go."

"Think about all that you have to go through to be with him. It's impossible to have anything stable with somebody who's already with somebody else—and as much as I hate to say it, Will might be the better candidate for you," Alisha told her friend.

"No way," Lindy disagreed, "God himself will have to marry me and Will. I just don't see that happening...you know, I was listening to what Deana said, but all of that was said in humor," Lindy continued, changing the subject. "Love your man, and respect your man too...I know that me and Darien are not the best of friends, but girl, I still want you to do what's right. As for me and Deana, we're single and we can only give you a single woman's perspective."

"Well, I'll be," Alisha said, surprised at Lindy's attitude.

"No, I'm serious! Don't get caught up in the conversation tonight," Lindy stressed. "If you were single it would be different, but seriously now, girl—you have to do what's right."

"Yeah...but it's hard sometimes," Alisha sighed heavily. "I think about being single...even though we just got married."

"Girl, have you lost your mind? Darien is nice-looking, has a good job, money in the bank and a 401(k) plan...he's helping you with school *and* your business, he took you out of that raggedy apartment and put you in this beautiful house...and you say *what* again?"

Alisha was silent.

"Alisha?"

"What?"

"Slap yourself!," Lindy said, "you *must* be crazy!"

"Well..."

"Well *nothing*, girl!," Lindy repeated. "Don't let this woman mess your marriage up. She's always talking about how good it is to be single; I'm single too, but I'm not always advertising it to you every possible chance I get."

"Me and Darien will be all right; it's okay," Alisha reassured Lindy.

"All I'm saying is, be careful...I really don't have a good vibe from Deana."

"Okay, Lindy," Alisha said, bypassing her friend's warning. As she drove up to Lindy's house, Lindy said, "Call me when you get home."

"Okay," Alisha replied. Lindy got out closed the door. As Alisha drove off she turned the radio up and began to sing to keep from falling asleep.

Darien looked at his watch and noticed that it was 1:20am, and he had not had a call from Alisha; he tried to call her on her cell, but there was no answer. Darien got up from the couch and went back to the bedroom. He took off his shirt and laid down across the bed. About 15 minutes later, Alisha turned the front door knob and came into the darkened house. She walked back to the closed bedroom door and opened it, putting her purse on the dresser. As she began to take off her shoes, Darien rolled over and looked at her.

"Do you know what time it is?," he asked disapprovingly.

"I'm sorry, I got carried away and I wasn't watching the time," Alisha apologized. "Baby, I'm really, *really* sorry."

"Alisha we've already had this conversation several times, over and over again," he said, in no mood to accept her apology. "I'm not letting you intentionally disrespect me anymore—I'm tired of it. Why don't you get some married friends? Obviously, your single friends don't respect or understand what's going on with me and you."

"It's not that. It's not Lindy; it's just that I got back here too late, and I really intended to be home way earlier than this."

"Where did you go?"

"I went to a friend's party..."

"Oh, so you weren't with Lindy," Darien said.

"Yes, I was with Lindy—but we were invited to a party by a friend," Alisha tried to explain.

"What friend?," he asked suspiciously. "I don't know of any 'friend'...so now you have secret friends that I don't know about? Oh I get it, it must be a man."

Darien's tone was an accusation. Alisha exhaled angrily.

"No! It was *not* a man. It was just a friend of mine I met at the shop, her name is Deana."

"Great! Just great—somebody *worse* than Lindy! I don't think I can handle yet another bad influence on you," Darien said.

"What do you mean, *another* bad influence?," Alisha demanded. "These are my friends—and I feel like it should be *my* choice as to who I hang out with. Darien, I'm tired of you controlling me! I am independent, I have my own money, and I can do whatever I want to do...I'm tired of you controlling my life. *You* tell me who I can hang out with, *you* tell me where I can go...and I don't like it!"

Alisha's pent-up feelings continued to pour out. "Why does it always have to be about what you want from me, shouldn't you be concerned about some of the things that

I want? I know you are the man of the house and all of that, and I respect that; but Darien, I am my own woman! I try my best to be a good wife, but I can't do it if you're always controlling me." Darien looked at her questioningly.

"Where is all this coming from, Alisha? This doesn't even sound like you; this must be something Lindy has put in your head, and you're trying to act it out," he stated. "I'm not trying to control you, all I am saying is you're not single anymore—and you *can't* do whatever you want to do. Neither can I! It seems like the more you hang out with her, the more you *become* her."

"Whatever," Alisha said, which angered Darien.

"What do you mean, 'whatever'?" Darien got up out of the bed and walked up to Alisha.

"Oh, so now you're gonna hit me?," she asked in disbelief. "Is that what you do, walk up on me and hit me?!"

Alisha put her finger in Darien's face. "If you touch me, one of us is going to jail, and the other is going to the emergency room." Darien stared, noting his wife's slurred speech. "You are drunk," he said.

"Whatever...I'm not drunk." Alisha took off her clothes and got into bed. Darien got back in the bed, moving further over to his side. As Alisha rolled over to her side of the bed, she picked up her phone from the nightstand and began to send text messages to Deana and Lindy to let them know that she had made it home safely. Darien rolled back over, annoyed once again.

"Who are you texting in the middle of the night?"

"Lindy and my other friend from the shop, Deana," she answered.

"Why are you acting all brand-new?," he demanded, puzzled with his wife's behavior; but Alisha gave no response. She rolled over and closed her eyes.

"So...you have nothing to say." Darien paused for a few seconds then rolled over, facing away from Alisha. "Just forget it," he muttered. Darien laid in the bed and thought to himself, *Chicago, here I come...I can't wait to leave. I'm getting all the details first thing in the morning; I'll show her two can play this game!* On the other side of the bed, Alisha was drifting off to sleep; the replies from her text messages began to come back to her from Lindy and Deana. She took her phone and put it on 'silent' and read Deana's text message.

You guys left too soon-- the party's just getting started

Alisha didn't reply; she put the phone back on the nightstand and drifted off to sleep.

Chapter 3

Birds of a feather flock together

The next morning Darien got up at his normal time. He made coffee and rushed out the door without waking Alisha. He called back about an hour later to wake her up. Alisha answered the phone.

"Hey, baby!," she said, but Darien had no enthusiasm in his voice.

"Hey. I was just calling to wake you up, now I have to go," he said.

"Baby wait, do you have to get off the phone like that?"

"I'm just busy," Darien replied, "I'll talk to you later."

"Well...all right then baby, I'll talk to you later," Alisha said, and hung up the phone. "Wow!," she said to herself, stunned by Darien's brush-off.

She sent Darien a text message and said, *you didn't have to be that rude to me. I understand that you're mad at me, but please give me the respect that you would want if the shoe were on the other foot.*

Alisha got out of the bed stretching and yawning, then put on her house robe and walked into the kitchen. She got a cup of coffee, went to the living room, turned on the TV and started to watch the news. She heard her phone ringing in her bedroom and got up and go get it and bring it back to the living room. She checked all the missed calls and she noticed that she had a call from her mom's house. *I'll call her back later,* she said to herself. Moments later, she got a call from Deana; she answered.

"Hey girl, what do you have planned around about 11 o'clock?," Deana asked.

"Not a whole lot," Alisha replied. "My first appointment for today isn't till 1:30p.m., but right now I'm just watching TV and drinking some coffee...what do you have planned?"

"Let's go shopping."

"I don't have any money for shopping, but I tell you what, I can watch you shop."

"Okay, I'll meet you at your shop—that way, you can drop your car off and ride with me. I need to go to the mall and exchange some things I bought," Deana said. "Girl, I bought some jeans, and I don't know what I was thinking. I wanted a pair of jeans so bad, I bought them anyway—even though I knew they were not my size," she laughed.

"I've been there before," Alisha said, "I remember buying a pair of jeans one time, just so this other lady in the store couldn't get them." Deana laughed.

"It was almost a fight in Macy's," Alisha continued, "and I still have those jeans today—and I cannot wear them!"

"Okay, I'll pick you up around 11 o'clock at the shop, and we'll have a little brunch."

"Fine! I'll call you as soon as I get there."

"Okay, see you then."

About 10 minutes later, Deana called back.

"Can you touch my hair up?," Deana asked. "I sweated my hair out last night, and you know when we go to the mall I have to be on point—there might be some young cowboys there looking for a black stallion."

Alisha laughed and said, "okay, I got you."

After hanging up the phone, Alisha looked at the clock and noticed it was about 9:15a.m. She grabbed a few of her schoolbooks, laid on the couch, and began studying. A short while later Alisha got dressed and left the house, heading for the beauty shop.

Deana walked through the door at the beauty shop at 11:15a.m.

"Sorry I'm late, girl—traffic was backed up," Deana apologized.

"It's okay. Go on, sit down in the chair—I want to turn on some music." Alisha left the room briefly. "So, you just want a touch up, right?"

"Yes," Deana replied. She looked at herself in the mirror and ran her fingers through her hair. "My hair looks really bad, please do something to it."

Alisha gave Deana a quick, stylish hairdo; once she'd finished, she said, "I don't know if I'll be able to go with you, because I won't have enough time to get back before my 1:30 appointment."

"Is there any way possible you can adjust your schedule?," Deana asked. "I really want you to go with me."

"I don't know, I'll see...let me give them a call." Alisha called her 1:30 appointment and was able to reschedule it to 3:30. "All clear," Alisha said as she got off the phone.

"That's great," Deana said as she checked herself out in the mirror.

"Let me cut off the music, and then we can leave," Alisha said to her.

"Okay." A call came through on Deana's cell phone; almost immediately, she began to argue with the person on the other end of the line. The argument escalated, and Deana abruptly hung up the phone.

"Are you alright?," Alisha asked.

"Yes," Deana answered, still obviously upset. "I'm just tired of people getting on my nerves; you ask them to do one thing, and they feel as if they can do what you ask them to do *their* way...I'm sick of people that cannot follow directions or use common sense! I think I'm going to fire my assistant; this person consistently drops the ball, and I just can't have that." Deana looked at Alisha. "Do you want to be my assistant?," she asked.

"I wish I could; but I don't know if I can work for you...I don't want to drop the ball, and have you start choking *me* out," Alisha said.

"I wouldn't choke you up," Deana laughed. "I wouldn't do you like that—you're my girl. Furthermore, you're way more competent than my assistant," she said as she pulled into a parking space at the mall. Deana put her car in 'park'. "Are you ready, Alisha?," she asked.

"I'm ready to shop till we drop," Alisha said.

Walking through the mall, Deana said to Alisha, "I should've brought some different shoes; my feet are hurting already."

"That's what you get for trying to be sexy all the time." Deana sighed. "You're right." As they strolled through the mall Deana told Alisha about everything that went on at the party after she and Lindy left.

"By the way, where is Lindy?"

"I don't know," Alisha said. "She hasn't called me today, that's not like her. I'm sure she has some wild story to tell me of how the rest of her night went."

"I saw her talking to that guy last night at the party; I don't think he is a good person to talk to," Deana said. "I've heard some things about him, word-of-mouth, that are not really good."

"I'm sure Lindy is going to get the 411 on him," Alisha said. "Do you see those shoes over there in the window? I've got to go see if they have those in my size," she said, changing the topic. They walked into the shoe store and the salesman came over.

"Hi, can I help you?," he asked.

"Yes, can I see the shoes that are in the window on display In a size 7, please?," Alisha asked.

"Sure, I'll be right back—I'll see if I still have it in that size."

While waiting, Alisha picked up another shoe from the display. "I have to have this shoe," she said. Looking at the bottom of the shoe, she changed her mind. "Not for $250...I like it, but I don't like it *that* much," she said.

"This is nice, but I like the shoe over here," Deana said; "have you seen this one?"

Another shoe salesman came up to Deana and said, "I already know—you need that in a size 8."

"You're right," Deana smiled.

"I'll be right back with your shoe," the salesman said, "is there anything else I can get you while I'm back there?" The salesman pulled another shoe from the display and showed it to Deana. "Have you seen this nice black shoe? It will really look good on your feet, and it looks classy." Deana liked what she saw.

"Yes," she said, "can you grab that from the back as well? 'Cause I'm a classy lady, and I do like that shoe."

"I like the shoe you were just looking at—it has your name written all over it," Alisha remarked.

"Yes—at $350, it *should* have my name written all over it," Deana agreed. "I have an outfit that I'll put that black shoe with, and I already know it will look so good together when I go to Atlanta for this party/ business meeting soon. The who's-who of the city will be there; you want to come with me? I normally take my assistant...but *you* should come with me."

"I don't know...I'm unsure if I'll have the extra money to go," Alisha said, "and I know my husband would hit the ceiling if he knew I was going to Atlanta."

"I didn't ask you for any money—if you want to go, let me know," Deana said. "I'll let you work it out with the old ball-and-chain."

"When are you leaving?," Alisha asked; her mind was at work, figuring out the details.

"In about three weeks, and I can't wait to get some chicken and waffles from Glades Knight's restaurant," Deana answered.

The salesman came back with their shoes. "Here you go, ladies; try these on," he said. They both thanked him as Alisha took her pair of shoes and Deana took hers. Alisha tried her shoes on and stood in the mirror to admire them.

"How do I look?," she asked.

"They look good on your feet," Deana said.

Deana tried hers on and stood in the mirror beside her; like at the party, Alisha felt a bit uncomfortable, because Deana was standing a little too close. *I guess everybody doesn't feel the same way about 'personal space'*, Alisha thought; she moved and went back to her seat to take the shoes off.

"You should get those, girl, they look really good on your feet," Alisha advised.

"You're right," Deana agreed. She picked up the shoes Alisha had tried on. "And I'm getting these," she told the salesman, "we are going to get these shoes."

"No—I don't have the money," Alisha protested.

"I got it," Deana insisted. She pulled out her American Express card and laid it on the counter.

"Did you find everything you were looking for?," the cashier asked.

"Yes."

"Your purchase today comes up to $ 678.98." The cashier took the card, rang up the purchases, and thanked Deana as she handed her the receipt.

"You didn't have to do that...I could've waited on those shoes, I—thank you," Alisha said and hugged Deana.

Walking in the mall, Alisha saw another shoe store a few stores down.

"We have to stop at this shoe store, they have unbelievable sales," she said excitedly. As they both walked into the shoe store, Alisha looked around and said, "I feel like I've died and gone to SHOE HEAVEN!!! Let me find size 7...girl, *look* at these shoes—they are better than the ones we got from the other store. I have to try on the display shoe in the window; I might have to write a faith check..."

Deana looked puzzled.

"You know what a faith check is, don't you?," Alisha asked. "A faith check is when you write a check and believe by faith that the money will be there when it goes through."

"Girl, you're crazy," Deana laughed, "faith check!" She laughed again.

Standing in front of the mirror, Alisha got the attention of other ladies who were passing by, and they began to admire the shoes Alisha tried on. All of a sudden, Deana's mood changed.

"Let's go—there's nothing in here for me...all the shoes in my size look 'ghetto'," Deana complained.

"You haven't even looked around yet," Alisha pointed out.

"I'm just ready to go," Deana said crossly. "The store has nothing for me."

Deana walked out of the store and stood in the hallway. She received a phone call, and started to talk with her back facing the store. *Wow...what's wrong with her?*, Alisha wondered. She took the shoe off and put it back on the display rack in the window.

"That shoe will look good on you," the salesman said, "is there something else I can help you find?"

"That's all right," Alisha said.

"You sure?," the salesman pressed, still trying to make a sale. "That one *really* looked good on your foot..."

"That's alright, I've gotta go."

"If you change your mind, I'll be at the counter," he smiled.

Alisha walked out of the store into the hallway and up to Deana as she talked on the phone.

"You alright?," she asked. Deana moved the phone away from her mouth and spoke.

"There was nothing but cheap stuff in there...we can find something better, let's go somewhere else." Deana then continued her conversation with her assistant.

"As soon as you have that information for me, call me back and let me know ASAP," she said. Deana turned to Alisha.

"Have you been to the new store that just opened up?"

"No, I haven't been to the mall in God-knows-when, I heard they have some unbelievable purses and shoes in that store."

As they got closer to the store, Alisha saw a lady from her church. They walked towards each other.

"Hello, Ms. Maxwell," Alisha said. Ms. Maxwell looked up, a surprised smile on her face.

"Hey, Alisha! I haven't seen you in a long time. How are things going with you?"

"Everything is fine, ma'am," Alisha replied.

"That's good," Ms. Maxwell said. "Who is your friend?," she asked.

"Oh, this is my friend Deana."

"Where are you two ladies on the way to?"

"We're on our way to see that new store that just opened up," Alisha answered. Ms. Maxwell shook her head.

"I just left out of there, and those prices are outrageous!," she said. "It's too rich for my blood—and those high heels are too high for me. I'm an old lady, that place is for you spring chickens," she chuckled. "Alisha, I heard you got married not too long ago."

"Yes ma'am," Alisha said proudly.

"Congratulations, dear; let me see the ring," Ms. Maxwell asked.

Alisha held out her hand and showed her the ring. Ms. Maxwell smiled.

"That is nice, I'm really happy for you, baby. You are a young lady, and I'm an old lady; and I know this is advice that you did not ask for, but I'm going to give it to you, if you want a successful marriage. Take it from me—I've been married to my husband for 40 years, and here's my secret: love him like you can't live without him, and respect him and honor him even when he makes mistakes."

"Yes, ma'am," Alisha said.

"Give me a hug," Ms. Maxwell said, embracing the younger woman. "I'll let you two go now, Alisha. I want to see you back at church; those kids miss you, and you need to come back to church…you know better, and you know the way."

"Yes, ma'am. I'm going to start back coming to church, because I do miss my church."

"Alright, I'm looking forward to it," she smiled again. "Bring your friend, too." Alisha said she would, and waved goodbye as she and Deana walked off. Deana looked at Alisha.

"I told you you were a church girl," she said, "now you got me feeling all bad for having you out the other night."

"We have no time to feel bad now," Alisha said, "you see the shoes in the display case up ahead?"

"I do! Girl, you might have to take a backseat on this—I've *got* to have those."

They went into the store, mesmerized by the shoes in the display case.

"Do you have the shoe in the window in a size 8?," Deana asked the salesperson.

"Yes I believe I do," the salesperson said—to Deana's delight. "Let me go get it for you, it just came in; a lot of people have asked about that shoe today."

"Yes, it is hot!," Alisha added.

While waiting on the salesperson to come back with Deana's shoe, Alisha and Deana walked around the store and browsed the purses. Deana's cell phone rang, and she quickly answered.

"Do you have that information?," she asked.

"Yes, I have everything taken care of for you," her assistant said. *"The flight and hotel reservations are taken care of."*

"Thank you very much. I'll see you when I get back to the office."

"Alright, 'bye."

Deana hung up, looking expectantly at Alisha.

"Remember when I told you that this trip to Atlanta was a business party?," Deana asked.

"Yes," Alisha replied.

"Well...you know I told you I was going to help you out and look out for you as much as I could, right?"

"Right...," Alisha said, hesitantly.

"Brace yourself!," Deana exclaimed, "I'm taking you with me to Atlanta! Believe it or not, I have a client in Atlanta who wants to show a promotional video for a product they're getting ready to release—and they're going to need a hairstylist for some of the models they'll be using; and *guess* who I recommended...?"

Alisha paused, already shocked at what she thought Deana would say.

"You!," Deana shouted.

"I...I'm speechless," Alisha said.

"Don't be speechless—say you will accept!"

"I don't have the money to go down there. And I *don't* want to put it all on you."

"If it will make you feel better, you can pay me back," Deana said. "I just want to open this door of opportunity to you; I know that you do a good job, and I have faith in you that you won't let me down—and this could lead to other opportunities for you as well, so think about the big picture! I know that you have to talk to your husband, but this is something that he should understand. This could definitely open up doors of opportunity for you."

Alisha pulled out her phone and sent a text message to Darien saying, *baby, it's important—we need to talk when you get home! I love you.* Alisha put her phone back in her purse and she and Deana began to shop.

"I guess we are now the Dynamic Duo, we've got to have something hot to wear to this party," Deana said enthusiastically.

"Yes, I definitely agree," Alisha said. About 45 minutes later, they met at the counter with their items and the salesperson began ringing up their purchases.

"Wait, let me get these earrings," Alisha said, as she brought them to the counter.

"Is that all? You sure you don't want to get anything else?," the cashier asked.

"Yes, that's it."

"Your total comes to $1,387.92." Deana gave the salesperson her credit card, and stood aside to take another phone call. Alisha decided to call and tell Lindy the good news about her going to Atlanta. While talking to Lindy, she noticed the time on her watch.

"I have to get back to the shop," she told Lindy, "my appointment will be there in about 20 minutes."

"Where are you?," Lindy asked.

"I'm with Deana at the mall, we grabbed a few things." Lindy frowned. "You don't have any money—where'd you get some money from? Alisha...don't you think it's strange that this random person you just met is spending all of this money on you?"

"We're just good friends," Alisha said defensively.

"Alisha, you just met her not too long ago! You don't have the time or the history with her to even say she's a good friend—and furthermore, what do you even know about her?"

"Lindy, why are you acting like this? Maybe I should just call you back later."

"Okay. I'm not saying this like it's all 'spiritual' or anything like that, but I *really* have a bad feeling about her."

"I'll just call you back," Alisha said abruptly, cutting off any further discussion of Deana.

"Alright...'bye." Lindy quickly hung up the phone. Deana walked up to Alisha, noting the troubled expression on her face.

"Is everything okay with you?," Deana asked.

"Yes. I'm fine," Alisha replied.

"Who were you talking to?"

Alisha hesitated, with that same strange look on her face.

"Nobody," she answered, blocking any further questioning. As they walked out of the store, Deana made a suggestion. "Before we leave, we have to get some ice cream," she said.

"I second that!," Alisha said. "I would love to have some butter pecan ice cream—it's my favorite. I love butter pecan ice cream."

"Really? Me too! I can eat butter pecan ice cream all day and all night." They walked up to the counter and placed their order.

"Pay for it, okay? I have to go to the restroom," Deana said.

"Okay, I've got it."

The young man behind the counter asked if Alisha would prefer cones or bowls, and Alisha requested that he put the ice cream in two bowls. The young man was just telling her the total, when a voice behind her said, "add a banana split onto the order."

Alisha turned around, and to her surprise, she was standing face-to-face with Marcus.

"So, we meet again," he said, in a deep voice.

"How are you?," she asked.

"I'm fine," he said. "How is married life treating you?"

"I'm fine."

Marcus reached into his pocket and pulled out a wad of cash. He gave the young man behind the counter a $10 bill to pay for Alisha's order, and they started walking away from the counter.

Who are you here with? Your husband?," Marcus asked.

"No, I'm here with a friend," Alisha replied.

"Good! Maybe you can introduce me to her, is she like you?," he joked. "I need a woman like you in my life—a good one."

"Actually, she's a great one—she has a lot of things going for her, and you all could make the perfect couple. She'll be out of the restroom in a minute."

No sooner than Alisha had spoken those words, Deana came around the corner; she walked up to Marcus.

"I know you," she said, a cautious tone in her voice.

"I know you, too," Marcus said, his voice equally guarded.

They paused for a second, sizing each other up. Alisha looked at both of them strangely; *what's going on?,* she wondered.

"Do you know him?," Deana asked Alisha.

"Yes," she answered.

"*This* is your friend?," Marcus questioned.

"Yes," she answered again, this time with a strange look on her face.

"Oh! I didn't know it was like that," Marcus smirked. "Well...I guess I'll be seeing you, Alisha." He turned around and walked away. Alisha turned to Deana, puzzled.

"I'm confused...what just happened?"

"If something happened that I was unaware of, then apparently you need to pick a better class of friends than him," Deana said.

"What's wrong with him? And why did you guys look like you were going to go for each other's throats as soon as you saw each other?," Alisha demanded. "Girl, I thought I was going to have to call somebody to pull you two apart!"

"You're almost right!," Deana admitted. "That man is evil. And I'm not saying that I'm a Christian who goes to church every Sunday, but I will say *that* man is going to burn in hell for some of the things he's done to people in this city." Deana continued. "I had a friend who ran a shelter for underprivileged families, and they did a lot of outreach to the community by providing jobs, shelter, and clothing for people in the neighborhood. Marcus and his father's company stole the building from under them, and tore it down—all for nothing. That man is a devil, and one day he's going to get what he deserves."

"Wow...I didn't know all of that. I just ran into him about a week ago—and I didn't know all of that was going on...wow."

"Yes—and I think he was looking at you with lust all in his eyes." She eyed Alisha cautiously. "You two never had anything going on, did you?"

Silly Women & Sleepy Men

"No! You know how you feel like a certain guy is 'the one that got away'?...well, that's how I had felt about him. Everybody has had that feeling, right?"

Deana turned up her nose in disgust. "You feel like that about *him*?! Please, let him go—he's not the one that got away, and I wouldn't wish that on my worst enemy. I'm telling you, that man is evil."

Walking back out to put their shopping bags in Deana's trunk she said, "Enough about him, girl you need to be focused on Atlanta. Now I can't wait to get down there! Think about all of the shopping we'll be able to do once we get down there..."

"Yes, Shoe Heaven all over again," Alisha sighed.

"What time is it?," Deana asked suddenly.

"Oh, no! Its 3:15...we really have to go."

They quickly got into the car; Deana said, "I'll get you there—but you might want to put on your seatbelt! This is going to be a bumpy ride..."

While at work, Darien looked at his phone for a second time; he was amazed at Alisha's text message.

"Tommy, man—I can't believe Alisha would send me a text message that says she wants to talk to me, she loves me...man, you know sometimes I really do believe that old saying: that Men are from Mars and Women are from Venus," Darien said. "She is really crazy! It's like the more I do for her, the less she appreciates it. I try to focus on providing for her school expenses, and that salon that's costing me a ton of money—and she *still* doesn't act right."

Darien was really on a rant, and gave Tommy an earful.

"Everything that she did last night—coming in late, then on top of that, she'd been out drinking—I really don't believe how she disrespects me. The story goes on; it's not over: now all of a sudden, she has friends that I don't know anything about...man, it seems like it's always something with this girl! Seems like the more I do, the less she cooperates."

"Maybe you guys just need a break from each other; just a little time to get away to refresh yourself," Tommy said, trying to be sympathetic. "Sometimes when you're together all the time and being under each other all the time, you can get agitated really quickly. Man, she's got you looking really bad—it's written all over your face."

"Thanks for taking me back to your 80's playlists," Darien said.

"No, I am serious," Tommy stressed, "you need a break—a change of scenery, just for couple of days—and Chicago looks like the perfect place."

"You know, Tommy, every now and then you are right. I *do* need to get away, the last few trips that I've taken, she's been with me."

"He's finally come into the light," Tommy joked, looking up to the sky.

"No, I'm for real. I think you're right. I tell you what; count me in on the Chicago trip—I'll even sit through the boring seminars."

"Good, because I already booked your room and Anthony owes me $10, because we had a bet going that you wouldn't go," Tommy laughed.

"You guys are unbelievable," Darien said, shaking his head.

"You are too! You just made me 10 bucks."

"And furthermore," Darien said, "how is Anthony going to Chicago, and he still hasn't paid me all of my money back from bailing him out of jail?"

"Man, you know Anthony is going to come up with some astronomical story."

"Yes that's true...well, we'll work it out later," Darien said, "but count me in—I definitely need to go; I need time to get away."

"Man, this is a money-making opportunity! I'm telling you, once you do this you will never be the same."

"Never be the same; man, you make it sound like it's church."

"It's the next best thing," Tommy declared.

Hey, I gotta go—I'll catch up with you later."

"Don't back out on us," Tommy said.

Three hours later Darien was riding home, contemplating all the words that he'd say to Alisha when he saw her. In the midst of his thoughts, a call came in from Alisha's mom; he answered the phone.

"Hello Mom," he greeted his mother-in-law.

"Son, how are you doing?"

"I'm doing just fine, everything is all right."

"That's good. I was calling for Alisha; I called her earlier, but she didn't answer her phone. That's highly unlikely for her not to answer the phone when I call."

"She's been doing a lot of new things lately," Darien said. "I don't know what's gotten into her, honestly, but I will definitely tell her to call you."

"Would you do that for me? Tell her Uncle Fred is sick and he's not doing well."

"Okay. I will make sure that I tell her as soon as I get home."

"Make sure you do—and pray for him."

"Yes ma'am, we definitely will."

"Okay, I'll let you go. I know you're a busy man, so I'll talk to you later; I love you."

"I love you too, Mom."

Darien got off the phone; as soon as he arrived home, he was greeted by his ever-watchful neighbor, Greg.

"How's it going?," Greg asked.

"Everything's fine. I'm just a little tired; I had a long day at work and I just can't wait to hit the bed. I am so beat..."

"I understand that feeling," Greg said, picking up on Darien's mood. "I'll check you out another time."

"Maybe we can get together and watch the game tomorrow," Darien offered.

Greg's eyes lit up. "Sounds good," he said. "Hey, I'll cook some of my world-famous jalapeno hot wings."

"Greg, the last time you cooked those wings, nobody could eat them! My mouth is *still* on fire," he joked.

"Why, thank you for such flattering words," Greg said, sarcastically.

"We'll talk about it tomorrow; I'm getting ready to go in."

"Okay, see you tomorrow."

As Darien walked into the quiet house, he thought to himself, *she must be working late.* He picked up the phone to call her, but thought better of it; *no, I'm not going to call her.* He walked in the kitchen, looked in the refrigerator, and poured himself a glass of juice. "Boy, I'm hungry," he said, gazing into the refrigerator while trying to find something to eat. Giving up, he closed the door and said, "well, I guess it's fast food tonight." He got back in his truck and drove to a fast food restaurant. While he was in the drive-through lane, he called Alisha. She picked up the phone.

"Hello baby, have you eaten already?," Darien asked.

"I'm a little hungry," Alisha said.

"Since you weren't at home, I stopped at a fast food restaurant to grab something for us to eat."

"That's cool. Make sure you bring me some onion rings back—I already know where you are," she said.

"Okay."

"I'll be home in about 30 to 45 minutes."

"Okay, see you," Darien responded.

"I love you," Alisha said.

It was an awkward moment; Darren was slightly hesitant to say, *"I love you, too"* ; and finally said, "alright...I almost forgot to tell you, your mom called me today and said she'd been trying to call you, but you have not answered your phone. She said it's important, it's about your Uncle Fred."

"Okay. I'll make sure I call her back right now."

"Okay...I'll see you when you get home."

Alisha said goodbye and hung up the phone.

While Darien was making his way home with the food, Alisha had wrapped things up with her last client at the shop, and was also on the way home. She called her mother.

"Hi Mama, what's going on?," Alisha said. "You called Darien and he said it was important, what is it? Are you all right?"

"I'm fine, but it your Uncle Fred," her mother replied. "He's gotten sick, baby...and he does not have long, according to the doctors. You need to come and see your uncle. I know it's been a long time since you all spoke, and I know what happened."

"I'll try my best to come down there and see him," Alisha said indifferently. "I know he's my uncle, but Mama, you *know* how I feel about him."

"I know, baby...but we're still family—and if you don't do it, I'll have to get somebody else to get down there and visit him for me."

"Okay, Mama—I'll do the best that I can," Alisha said, "I gotta go, talk to you later..."

"*Alisha!,*" her mother interrupted her. "Don't be stubborn; *do it for your Mom.*"

"Okay, Mom! As soon as I have time I'll come down there...I have to let you go now," Alisha said, and hung up the phone.

As she drove home, Alisha began to have flashbacks from her childhood...of her and Uncle Fred.

"Please take this away from me!," she said out loud, "take the memories away from my mind, I can't take it."

She thought about all of the stresses that were on her, and right in the midst of feeling down, Lindy called.

"What's going on, are you still out with your new BFF?," Lindy asked in a nice-nasty voice. Alisha sighed, ignoring Lindy's dig.

"No. I'm on my way home to deal with Darien," she replied. "God knows I don't feel like dealing with him tonight; I know he's still mad from last night, and he's been real snappy with me all day."

"I tell you how to get out of these situations all the time," Lindy said simply, *"you need those red boots—how are you going to be married, and not give it up?!"*

"Look Lindy, don't start. I'm really going through a lot."

"Maybe that's why!," Lindy said.

"Girl, stop..."

"You need to relax, relate, and release."

"I'm not even in the mood for all of that," Alisha said. Lindy exhaled loudly, frustrated with her friend's defeated attitude.

"It makes me not want to get married, if I've got to stop having fun and loving life—I'll pass!," she told Alisha. *"You are always depressed about something."*

"Well...it's not really Darien; I just got a call from my Mom, and she told me my Uncle Fred is sick."

"*Are you talking about the uncle that you told me about a long time ago?*"

"Yes," Alisha answered quietly.

"*Has that issue ever been resolved?*"

"No...even now, that situation has never been addressed or resolved; I just moved on."

"*That's serious. This might be a good opportunity to bring some closure, and to get healed from that whole situation, Alisha...you cannot carry that all of your life.*"

"Thank you, 'Bishop Lindy'," Alisha said, trying to make light of her friend's words.

"*No—I'm serious,*" Lindy stressed. "*I don't think I know everything, however, I am right on this: you can't carry unresolved issues around, Alisha—you've got to get rid of them. You can't always be quiet and reserved and take things in. Remember, Pastor Jones would tell us 'exposure brings closure'—the faster you can bring it out and talk about it, the faster you can get healed from it and move on.*" Lindy spoke on. "*Alisha...all I'm saying is, don't let the man pass away before the issue is resolved.*"

"I just don't want to deal with it, Lindy. There are some things that I didn't tell you about—some of the things in my childhood—and I just don't want to deal with it."

"*Alisha, you can't live your life closed; nothing new will enter if you lived your life closed.*"

"Where is all of this coming from, Lindy?"

"Pastor Jones," she replied quickly. "I _do_ pay attention to him when I'm in church."

"Lindy, you haven't been to church in almost 6 months!"

"I'm still right. You still need to deal with that."

"Well I made it home now," Alisha sighed, "and I am going to call you later. I might need another place to stay, because my husband might put me out after everything I did yesterday."

"Yeah, you do that...call me back later."

Alisha got off the phone as she pulled into the driveway. Bowing her head, she whispered, "Lord, help me."

She got out of the car and walked up to the house, carrying the bags from her earlier shopping spree with Deana. She stepped through the door with the bags and called out, "honey, I'm home"; Darien answered, "hey" from the kitchen. Alisha breathed a sigh of relief, noticing that she had a clear passage straight to the bedroom to put away the bags; but as she tried to ease past the kitchen, Darien's voice stopped her in her tracks.

"Wait a minute, stop right there...where did these bags come from?," he questioned her.

"Well...I did pick up a few things from the mall," she said.

"Oh...the mall," Darien repeated, waiting for Alisha to provide more details.

"I went out with my friend; you know, the one I was telling you about earlier, Deana."

"Now, where did you say you met her again?"

"I told you, she's a client of mine," Alisha replied.

"So, now you just go out with random people?"

"No," she answered flatly.

"You were just out with this lady last night...and now, she takes you shopping? I don't know, this doesn't sound right to me," Darien said.

"Darien, I have nothing to hide from you," Alisha said impatiently. "I was with Deana. I'm *not* cheating on you, and I'm not messing around, or anything else."

Darien started looking at the names on the bags she'd brought in.

"This stuff is expensive...I've got clients, they don't buy me expensive gifts like this," he said, "and furthermore, I thought you were studying for tests? So now, do I *really* have to talk to you like a parent—'don't let your friends get you in trouble so you don't finish your homework'?," Darien asked sarcastically.

"Don't worry about that, I have all of this under control," she said confidently. "Let me go set this stuff down and take my shoes off; I'll come right back to the kitchen, and we can talk."

Alisha walked away, taking the bags with her. She hollered back into the kitchen, "Baby, warm my food up, please—I'm hungry."

"Tell Deana to do it," Darien muttered under his breath, and Alisha vaguely overheard him.

"What did you say?," she asked.

"I'll be glad to do it," Darien said loudly.

Alisha changed clothes and joined Darien in the kitchen.

"I'm so hungry," she said, grabbing the burger and starting to eat. She sat down with Darien and began to tell him about her day.

"Darien, have you heard anything about Marcus and some outreach building that his father's company shut down?," Alisha asked.

"I heard a little bit about it; why do you ask?"

"Something funny happened to me and Deana today at the mall; we bumped into Marcus but when the two of them made eye contact, I thought I was going to have to call security," Alisha explained. "All of this hostility came out of nowhere, from both of them; it was kind of weird."

"Maybe they were lovers," Darien said. "Maybe they've been together before, and it didn't work out."

"Maybe," Alisha replied, deep in thought. "I asked further about it, and Deana just went into this story of Marcus shutting down an outreach building of a friend of hers. She went into 'it wasn't right', and all of that."

"Let's watch a little TV," Darien suggested, trying to change the subject; but Alisha said, "hey, there's something else I wanted to talk to you about."

"What? Where are you going to now?"

"Nowhere baby," she said with a serious look on her face.

"Still, I know what that means—it means that you want to do something. Alisha, we have the money to do whatever it is that you're trying to do," Darien stated.

"No, that's not it—I don't need any money; actually, an opportunity has opened up where I can actually make some money."

"How are you gonna do that, with all the things that we have going on here at the house?"

"Remember when you said I was stressed out and I needed to take a break?," Alisha asked.

When did I say that?, Darien thought to himself. "Yeah," he responded anyway.

"Well...I found the perfect opportunity today for me to get away and make some money at the same time," Alisha said.

"What are you talking about?"

"Deana is going to Atlanta for a business gathering, and they will have models there and she wants to use me as their stylist. What do you think about that, baby?"

"Alisha, I really don't know," Darien said, rolling the idea over in his mind. "How are you all going to get there?"

"By plane."

"Is she going to pay for the tickets too?"

"Yes, she already took care of that."

"This new friend of yours must have a lot of money," Darien wondered.

"I don't know the girl's bank account, but one thing I do know: whatever she does, she does it big."

Darien was unimpressed.

"The more I hear about this person, I really don't think I'll like her," Darien said.

"Why?," Alisha demanded, "because she's not broke and she does what she wants to do? Because she's independent? Darien, you need to come out of the Stone Age. You are like that about every woman who is independent."

"That's not true," Darien said defensively. "I just have a bad feeling about her."

"Well Darien, I need to let her know something by tomorrow. I would have thought you'd like me going to Atlanta to do this event."

"How long you planning to be gone?"

"Maybe three days, tops."

As he thought about it, Darien's mood changed; he had something to run past Alisha, too.

"Okay, that's fine," he agreed finally. "You're going to Atlanta, baby. I want to let *you* know that I want to go to Chicago with Tommy to check out a business seminar with him. It will be a good chance for *me* to get away, because I've been working and working and working...and I haven't had the opportunity to have any fun, or go out with my friends, either."

It was as if they switched roles, and Alisha started to interrogate him.

"How long will you be gone?"

"Just a few days."

"Who-all are going with you?," she quizzed.

"Tommy and Anthony," Darien answered.

"Always the Three Musketeers," she commented. "So you're just going to Chicago to hang out with them; why are you trying to get out of the city to hang out with them?,"

"No—I'm going to the *business seminar.* I'm trying to find out how to make some more *mone*y for us," he stated.

"So, that's the brochure you've been reading."

"Yes, I've been reading up on it, because Tommy is really riding my back about me going to the seminar. He says it's possible that you can even triple some of the money you put into the business. I've tried to thoroughly check it out before I do anything, because I can't afford to waste money on any schemes or get-rich-quick plans. I don't have the time or the money for that."

"Before you do anything, Darien, please let me know."

"I'm just going to listen," he assured her. "I'm not planning to do anything when we go."

"When do you plan on leaving?"

"In about three weeks."

"How you guys getting up to Chicago?"

"We're planning to drive."

"So...you already had everything planned out, without even talking to me first," Alisha said, a hint of accusation in her voice. Darien wasn't having it, though.

"Alisha, don't try to switch it around on me; *you* are the one who already has another job out of town—with a secret friend that I know nothing about," he said matter-of-factly. Alisha backed down, knowing Darien had a point.

"Well, I guess you can go—but don't do anything crazy with that Anthony. In all honesty, I really don't trust him."

Darien looked at her squarely. "Maybe it's not about you trusting him—it's about you trusting me, baby. Nothing is going to happen."

###

Early on Sunday morning, about a week later, Alisha got up and told Darien, "maybe I want to go to church today."

"Go ahead," Darien mumbled, still groggy.

"No, I want both of us to go to church," she insisted.

"Baby," Darien said, slightly raising his head off the pillow, "we have enough church in the DVD rack...why don't you go put on one of those DVDs? Or better yet, it's Sunday morning—just flip the channels, you will find all types of churches on TV...Alisha, I'm going back to sleep."

"Come on, Darien. I wanted you to go with me; we haven't been in so long, and Pastor Jones called me a couple of weeks ago...I feel really bad that I haven't been back to church yet."

"Go ahead," Darien repeated.

"No, I want both of us to go, baby."

"I'm tired, and I don't feel like going," Darien sighed. "It is nothing against Pastor Jones, but I'm just tired—I don't feel like it."

"Darien, if you're not out of this bed by the time I come back in this room, I'm coming in here with a cup of water to pour on you! We are going to church whether you like it or not," Alisha declared.

Darien laid back on the pillow and closed his eyes.

"Girl, if you pour some water on me, you're going to definitely need Jesus, and a few paramedics too—now, go in there, watch TV, and leave me alone. I am sleepy."

Alisha put her hands on his shoulder and shook him.

"Take up your bed and walk," she said jokingly.

"Get thee behind me Satan, I shall not be moved," Darien answered.

"Get up!," Alisha said, hitting Darien with a pillow.

"Girl, stop!," he complained.

Alisha hit him again with the pillow.

"Alisha, is there a story in the Bible where Jesus went to sleep on a boat?"

Alisha thought for a second; "yeah," she answered.

"Well, touch your neighbor and say 'I am stunning like my daddy!' I just took you to church," Darien said, "now please let me go back to sleep."

"Darien," Alisha said, seriously, "I really want to go—and I don't want Pastor Jones looking at me over his glasses."

"I'll make you a deal; what time is it now?"

"It's nine o'clock."

"I'll tell you what: if you let me sleep till 10:15, I'll get up and put my clothes on quickly; we'll only be a little late for church—and *everybody* will be happy."

"I'm waking you up at 9:45," Alisha insisted.

"Okay," Darien compromised. "Until that time, can you cook me a little breakfast, since you are getting me out of the bed early on my off day?"

"Darien, I want to start going back to church," Alisha said, but Darien gave no reply.

Alisha walked out of the bedroom and went into the living room. She turned on the TV and found a gospel music video station to listen to as she cooked. She went back into the kitchen and got out the eggs and bacon; as she started cooking, she also got a taste for pancakes but thought to herself, I *don't have enough time to cook pancakes*. She saw that it was its 9:40a.m.

"Darien, get up!," Alisha hollered back to the bedroom, but Darien was fast asleep. She put the plates on the table and went back to get Darien out of bed; she stood over him and began to shake him.

"Darien, get up."

"Give me 10 more minutes, I promise I'm getting up out of the bed," he mumbled into the pillow.

Alisha sighed, finally accepting the inevitable.

"That's it!," she said, "I'm leaving—I'm going without you." She went ahead and got ready for church.

"I'm getting ready to leave, Darien," she said before walking out of the house.

"I'll see you when you get back," he said.

"No you won't, because I'm going to my Mom's house."

"Well...call me when you get out of church, and I'll go down there with you, if you want me to."

"Okay, I'll call you," she said. "Your food is in the microwave."

"Thanks, I'll get it later."

Alisha went outside, got in her car, put the key in the ignition...and she realized she needed to stop on the way to church and get gas. Putting in a favorite gospel CD, Alisha looked at the clock and her heart sank. It was 11:20am; *man, I wanted to hear the choir sing,* she thought to herself, *but I am just entirely too late—and I still have to get gas.* Two blocks away from the house, she noticed that she'd left her purse at home. She turned the car around and went back home to get it. She dashed into the house and grabbed her purse from the bedroom dresser, noticing that Darien was still sleep. She dashed out of the door and hopped back into the car, frustrated. *I'm entirely too late,* she thought again, but another inner still voice said, *press on, anyway.*

Minutes later as she was getting gas at the station, Alisha received a phone call from Deana.

"What's going on girl, what are you doing today?," Deana asked.

"Nothing, just on my way to church," Alisha replied, "running a little late...what's going on with you?"

"Nothing. Just checking on you, trying to see how you're doing," Deana said. *"Well...call me when you get out of the house of worship."*

"What are you doing later, around about one o'clock?"

"Nothing."

"Well, I'll give you a call—I'm going to drive out to my Mom's house," Alisha said. "It's about an hour away."

"Let me know if you need somebody to ride with you, are you going by yourself? Or are you taking Darien with you?"

"I don't know if he really wants to go. I'll call him when I get out of church and if he doesn't want to go, you can ride down there with me."

"That sounds great, just let me know."

"Okay," Alisha said, hurrying back into the car after gassing up. As she pulled into the church parking lot, Alisha looked at the clock; it was 11:45. *I am super-late now,* she thought, *this is unbelievable.* As Alisha walked into the church she was greeted and hugged by Ms. Betty, one of the ushers at the door.

"Alisha, I haven't seen you in a long time," she smiled. "Where have you been?"

"I have been working, Ms. Betty."

"Well I'm just glad to have you here! It's good to see you, you look good," the usher said approvingly.

"Thank you, Ms. Betty," Alisha said, appreciating Ms. Betty's welcome. As the choir sang, Alisha found a seat in the back and enjoyed their wonderful voices. Alisha stood along with the rest of the congregation as they sang praises to God in a familiar, traditional song. Hands were lifted all over the sanctuary as people began to cry out to God. As tears streamed down the faces of members of the congregation, Pastor Jones stepped to the podium.

"Saints of God, the presence of the Lord is here," he said with a loud voice and a sincere heart, "let us open up together and give God the loudest shout of praise we have!"

The congregation responded with a joyful shout that filled the room. He spoke again to the congregation.

"There are people in here who feel trapped by the things in their past," he said with a loud voice. "Don't let the devils in your past delete your divine destiny. Now, let us all open our mouths and give God a loud shout!"

The congregation responded, and the musicians began to play their instruments; the sweet sound of the organ solo filled the sanctuary, and Pastor Jones led the congregation into the presence of God.

Alisha lifted her hands and began to cry out, saying, "God, I will change my life! I want to get closer to you."

Ms. Maxwell came over to Alisha and hugged her.

"Everything's all right," she said soothingly, "God loves you no matter what. You are a daughter of God." She held Alisha even tighter.

"I just feel like I am so far away," she told Ms. Maxwell.

"But He still loves you, Alisha—and He said He would never leave you or forsake you...He will be with you always."

Ms. Maxwell took Alisha by the hand and guided her to the front of the church for special prayer at the altar. Pastor Jones came down out of the pulpit and began to pray with Alisha.

After the dismissal, Alisha approached Pastor Jones.

"Pastor," she said to him, "everything you said today, it seemed as if it was just for me."

"It was God speaking, I am just the vessel He uses," the pastor said humbly.

"Pastor...is it possible that I can speak with you in your office?"

"Sure, let me say goodbye to a few more people and I'll be back. Tell Deacon Mack to let you in my office, and I'll be there in just a minute."

Alisha waited in Pastor Jones office, and received a text message from Deana.

Church Girl, have you got out of church yet? , it said.

I will be out in about 20 minutes, Alisha replied.

Pastor Jones came into the office and sat down at his desk.

"What's been going on, Alisha? We haven't seen you in so long; it's good to see you. Where's your husband?," he asked.

"I tried to get him out of the bed today," Alisha admitted. "He would not budge, so I left him there."

"Tell him I missed him today."

"I will."

"It's written all over your face, Alisha...what's the problem?"

Alisha took a deep breath, exhaled, and looked her pastor in the eyes. She spoke.

"Pastor Jones, I want to talk to you about something that I've never talked to anybody about."

"I'm listening," he responded.

"Pastor...I've been dealing with something from the past that has really hindered my life," she began, "and it is really difficult for me to talk to somebody about this."

Pastor Jones brought in some Kleenex for Alisha as her eyes began to well up with tears.

"It's all right, go ahead and let it out. I'm here for you no matter what it is...I'm with you."

"When I was 12 years old, my Uncle Fred came to stay with us—and he would always look at me in a weird, strange way. When I would put my bed clothes on, he would always wait until my mom wasn't around and come in my room and make me hug him. He always called me nasty, and he would always tell me how ugly I was; he told me that I was the reason why my Dad left my Mom. He made me feel so worthless."

Alisha paused for a moment to wipe the tears from her eyes. Pastor Jones got up to give her a cup of water, then sat back down.

"Alisha, did you ever tell anybody about this?," Pastor Jones asked.

"No...I always felt like I was the reason why my mom was unhappy; I always felt like it was all my fault—and if I was to tell on Uncle Fred, he would have to leave; then it would be all my fault again," Alisha explained. "I was just so confused about what to do. I wanted it to stop, but I didn't want to cause any more trouble...Pastor Jones, the worst of all was the time in the kitchen."

"What happened in the kitchen, Alisha?"

"One day, my Mom was walking out of the door; she kissed me goodbye and said 'be good, don't give Uncle Fred any problems'. I said okay. About 20 minutes later, Fred was in the kitchen cooking and he asked me if I wanted to join him. To a degree, I didn't; but I guess I thought the kitchen was a safe place, because I knew there were certain rooms he wouldn't come in with me. The kitchen was a place where my Mom would sit at the table and read all the time, so to get away from him, I would either be outside or in the kitchen because I knew that's where Mom was, and he wouldn't come in there. But this one particular day, he wanted me to come in the kitchen with him because he wanted to show me how to cook eggs. I went in the kitchen with him and as he broke the yolks into the skillet, he gave me the spatula and told me to watch the eggs--he'd be right back."

The memories came alive for Alisha as she continued to speak.

"He said, 'keep your eyes on them, because they'll burn if you don't pay attention to them'. Moments later, he came up behind me...and touched me inappropriately. That's why, until this day, I hate the smell and the taste of eggs—it reminds me of that moment in my life all over again."

"Did you tell your mother about it?," Pastor Jones asked.

"Yes...but she didn't believe me," she said sadly. "She said Fred wouldn't do a thing like that—that I was making it all up, out of my mind. She said I was just mad because Fred was hard on me, and never let me get my way. It's 20 years later, and that issue was never resolved; and now he's sick. My Mom called me to come out there to see him, but I really don't know if this is the time to tell her what he did to me as a child. I don't want to add stress to the situation, and I'm still trying to get over and out of it myself. My husband doesn't even know about this situation," Alisha revealed. "I have to be honest and say that there are certain limitations that I put on my marriage because of the issues and the memory of what happened to me as a child. I honestly and openly admit that some things that I go through in my marriage is because of me...Pastor, tell me—how do I get out of the situation? I don't want to remember these things anymore; and I am so hurt by what he did to me...I want to tell my Mom what he did to me, but I don't want to hurt her—what do I do?"

"The first thing, Alisha, is it's not your fault. The best thing to do is to wait for the appropriate time and then have a one-on-one talk with your mom. And the next thing you do, more than anything, pray the prayer of release."

"What do I say?"

"You ask God to release you from this situation, regardless of what happens and regardless of what's said," Pastor Jones explained. "You have to forgive yourself for not speaking out; you can't hold this inside of you. Then, one of the most difficult things, is you have to forgive him. It's a difficult process; understand that it t work overnight, but with a lot of prayer you can get through this...Alisha, you're going to come out of this. Just hold your head up and believe God—you have to realize it. Remember one thing: Jesus didn't do anything to deserve the cross, but He endured it because it was a process to get us back to God. Alisha, sometimes we go through things in life and they seem unbearable; and you ask yourself, *what did I do to deserve this*? But the answer is it's just a process; so when you come out of this process, you're going to be better than you are now."

Pastor Jones got up from his chair and went over to Alisha to hug her.

"I love you," he said, "and if there's anything else I can do, let me know. I'll be here for you."

"Thank you, Pastor Jones. I thank God for you; you have no idea how much of a blessing you've been in my life."

Alisha left Pastor Jones' office and got in her car. She looked at her phone and saw that she'd received a text message from Darien. *Where are you?*, he texted.

I am just leaving church, do you want to ride with me down to my Mom's house? Alisha responded.

Can we go later on? I've got a few things I wanted to do.

Okay go ahead. I will get Deana to ride with me, I'll see you when I get back into town.

Okay then, Darien replied.

Right after her last text to Darien, Alisha called Deana.

"What's going on?," Deana asked.

"Nothing," Alisha said, "have you had anything to eat yet? I'm starving."

"No. How was church today?"

"Great!"

"You weren't in there were rolling around on the floor, were you?," Deana asked sarcastically.

"Girl, stop!," Alisha said.

"So, are you and your husband going out to eat?"

"He didn't come with me to church," Alisha replied, "I'm by myself."

"Are you still going down to your Mom's house?"

"Yes. I know my Mom has been at the hospital with my uncle, so I'm sure she didn't cook. We can stop and get something before we ride down there."

"Great!," Deana said. "I'm hungry."

After their meal, the waiter brought the bill to their table; Deana pulled her credit card out of her purse.

"Don't worry, I have it," she said.

"No, I have it," Alisha insisted. "You're always doing stuff for me, let me do something for you."

Alisha gave the waiter cash and slid Deana's credit card back to her.

"Well okay then, baller!," Deana said.

Alisha smirked; she stood up and left a tip on the table.

"Are you going to ride with me?," she asked Deana.

"I can drive you down there."

"No I had planned on it—I can drive down there."

"Okay, I'll tell you what: why don't we drop your car off by your house, then you can drive my car down to your mom's house."

"Okay, but I didn't want to burn up all of your gas."

"I'm all right on gas as long as you drive," Deana said, "and if you drive, I can go to sleep."

"Fine," Alisha said.

They both got into their cars and drove to Alisha's house to drop off her car. About an hour later, Alisha was driving and Deana awakened from her nap; she started talking to Alisha.

"Are we there yet?," she asked.

"We're a couple of minutes away."

"So, did you get the Atlanta trip worked out?"

"Yes. I talked to him about it, and I'm going—but let me tell you what happened when I told him!"

"What?"

"He was already planning to go to Chicago with some of his friends!," Alisha said, still amazed. "He says it's for some seminar thing...but I don't believe that. I believe his friends are getting him up there and getting him to do some dirt."

"Does he go to seminars all the time?," Deana asked.

"No! This is the first time."

"I don't know...sounds fishy. I know men, and I simply don't trust them—as a matter of fact, I don't even trust them when they're right in front of me," Deana stated. "If you turn your head for one second, they're looking at the next skirt that's walking by, making eye contact...men are worse than dogs. Think about it: even a dog will be loyal...but you know your husband. Are his friends single?"

"Yes," Alisha said, making a sour face, "and I can't stand one of his friends, Anthony...now *he's* a dog for real—well, like you say, worse than a dog. He hits on every woman he comes in contact with—and then when he gets caught up he tries to be with both of them, *and* gets them to agree with it!," she said, shaking her head in amazement. "He has another friend, Tommy. He's all right, I suppose...but I'm kind of worried about Tommy. I've never seen him with a woman, he's always by himself; and some of the clothes he wears makes me raise my eyebrow..."

Deana laughed. "So, your husband has a friend that's low down and another friend that is down low!"

"I never thought about it like that," Alisha chuckled.

"All I'm saying is, your chosen might come back from Chicago saying he wants to talk."

"Girl, stop it!"

"I'm just playing," Dean said. "But jumping back to the Atlanta trip—I can't wait to go! We're going to have so much fun; have you ever been to Atlanta?"

"Once, but I didn't get a chance to really get out and see anything."

"We're going to have so much fun," Deana repeated, "and make money at the same time! And before we leave there, I must take you to a place called Chops—you will never be the same once you've been there."

"What is it?," Alisha asked, her curiosity piqued.

"I would call it a restaurant, but that is an understatement," Deana said.

"Wow...it's that good, then..."

"I paid a pretty penny the last time I was there, but believe me, it was worth every bit of it."

"Well, I can't wait to try it!," Alisha said.

Moments later Alisha pulled up to her Mom's house, went up to the door, and knocked. Her cousin Shirley came and opened the door.

"Hi Alisha, I haven't seen you in so long! How have you been doing?," Shirley asked.

"I've been doing fine," Alisha replied.

"Where is your husband?," Shirley asked, looking towards the parked car.

"I didn't bring him with me this time."

"Well, you two come on in; I just cooked, and you're just in time...come on in."

"Cousin, I would love to," Alisha said as they walked into the house, "but I just ate, and we are stuffed. I want to introduce you to my friend, Deana."

"Hello," she said pleasantly, "how are you?"

"Just fine," Shirley answered, turning to lead them into the house. Deana leaned over to Alisha and whispered into her ear, "I see where all of the butt and hips comes from—it runs in the family."

Alisha laughed.

"You need to stop it, girl! I wish I could, but I can't get rid of it," Alisha said.

"No you don't," Deana said, and playfully slapped Alisha on the butt while Shirley was in the kitchen. Alisha walked to the back of the house.

"Where is Mama?," she asked her cousin.

"She's not here, she's probably at the hospital with my Daddy," Shirley said.

"Okay. We're going to go up to the hospital."

"Are you going to come back?"

"I'm not sure; I've got to get my friend back."

Alisha and her cousin hugged; she also hugged Deana, letting her know that she'd enjoyed making her acquaintance. Alisha and Deana got back out to the car and prepared to drive to the hospital.

"How do you work this fancy thing?," Alisha asked as she fiddled with the radio tuner. "I'm used to normal cars."

"I know, that's why I'm trying to 'upgrade' you," Deana teased, as she helped Alisha turn on the satellite radio. She started up the engine and they were on their way to the hospital.

"It's amazing that only my cousin was there—that almost never happens at my Mom's house," Alisha observed. "When I was growing up, there was always a lot of folks there."

"I didn't have that luxury of having a whole lot of friends and family," Deana said, thinking back over her own life. "I was raised by my aunt—and she was somewhat of the outcast of the family because of some of things she did."

"What happened to your parents?," Alisha asked.

"My parents died in a car wreck when I was 10 years old."

"I'm sorry to bring that memory back up for you," Alisha said, full of remorse.

"It's okay...I deal with it. I just drown myself in my work and school to relieve the pain."

There was a heavy silence in the car for a few seconds, then Deana spoke again.

"When I was 13 years old I prayed a prayer to God...and he actually heard me and answered it," she began. "I hated my father, I hated him with a passion. My father was a very popular man; everybody knew him, everybody respected him, everybody loved him. I saw my father do things with other women, and my Mom never said anything. Some of the situations she knew about; and I hated her for that, too. One night my father came in; he was so drunk...he sat on the couch and turned the TV up so loud, it woke me out of my sleep. I came downstairs...he turned his head and looked at me, and said, 'baby girl, come over here'. He sat me on his lap and began to talk to me...he said to me, 'I love you', and he held me real tight."

Deana paused for a moment, taking a deep breath before she continued speaking. "He kissed me...and then he started kissing me even more, and harder; as I tried to push him off me, he got more aggressive. Then he got really angry because I hated what he was doing. I was only defending myself...but he took his belt off and began to beat me. I screamed for my Mom to help me, but she didn't hear me; she never came for me. He beat me with all his might. He put his hand over my mouth; then he laid on top of me and told me to shut up...after that night, he apologized to me—then the next day, he did it all over again. My Mom saw the blood on my bed sheets and I told her what happened; but she didn't believe me...she said 'your father would never do a thing like that' and 'don't you ever say anything like that about your father'. She was so blinded by what he was, she couldn't see what he had done. She just chose to ignore it. I believe she knew every time that man touched me," Deana said bitterly. "She didn't say anything because of her own self-esteem and the way she felt about herself. So that's why I live my life the way I do—nobody cares about me, and I don't care about anybody."

"I care about you; you're like my new best friend," Alisha said quietly. "This is a really transparent moment, because my Uncle Fred who we're going to see in the hospital—he molested me. And it's taken everything in me to come up here and see him. Not only because my Mom doesn't even know what happened, but because I never told anybody and I just repressed everything that happened. I just dealt with it throughout life."

"Maybe you should tell her," Deana suggested.

"It's not the right time. I am going to talk about it at the right time—at least, that's what my pastor said: to talk to my mother at the right time."

"I almost wish I wasn't going there now, knowing that he did that to you," Deana said. "I would love to meet your mother but I can't stay, knowing what happened to you; so I'm just going to be outside in the hall—knowing me, I might say something."

"Hold yourself together," Alisha urged. She put the car in 'park' and they got out of the car. As they walked up to the entrance of the hospital Deana said, "give me the keys, because I might need to come back down here to get something." With a serious look on her face, Alisha handed her the keys.

"Deana, don't go in here and act crazy," she said. "I need your support."

"Okay," Deana agreed.

Moments later in the hospital in room, Alisha was talking to her mother. Despite the stress of the situation, mother and daughter found it easy to connect. Alisha's mother asked how things had been going; and Alisha introduced her mom to Deana. Alisha's earlier concerns about what Deana might do faded away when she saw how Deana and her Mom began to instantly connect. Deana made conversation with her easily, telling her about all her accomplishments. Alisha's mother was impressed.

"That's good, I know you will motivate my baby to do same," she said.

About an hour later as Alisha and Deana got ready to go, her Mom said, "let's all have a word of prayer with Fred before you leave."

After their prayer, Alisha's mom walked with them out in to the hallway.

"Mama, I have something really important to talk to you about. I'll come back down real soon so we can discuss it," Alisha said.

"You can talk to me right now; I have time."

"No; this is not the right time." Alisha hugged her mother. "I love you," she said, and kissed her.

"Whenever you want to talk, Alisha, just let me know. I'm always here for you."

"Okay, Mama—talk to you later."

Riding the elevator down to the lobby, Deana told Alisha, "you really held yourself together very well."

"I know—I had my girl with me," she said, hugging Deana. "I thank you for coming with me; this was really difficult."

"It's no problem. I wouldn't have missed it for anything in the world."

"Let me get some water before we get back into the car," Deana said as they got out of the elevator.

"Can you get me some ice tea? I'm a little thirsty myself." Later on as they rode home, Alisha asked Deana, "can you come to my house? I want to introduce you to my husband, and maybe we can sit down and watch a movie or something like that."

"Sounds good. If it's cool with your husband, it's cool with me."

"It's cool," Alisha said. "He wants to meet you anyway, because he thinks it's some strange person I'm going out with every time I say your name."

Moments later, they drifted into a conversation about sex.

"You guys have been together for couple of years, right?"

"That's right."

"I want to know—is the fire still there?," Deana asked.

"I still love him," Alisha replied.

"No, I'm talking about sex; are you getting it on the regular?"

"Somewhat," Alisha said hesitantly, "but I'm always tired...between work and school, I'm just so stressed out that I really don't have that fire like I used to have. Back when we first got together, that man couldn't stop thinking about me; but now, sometimes I feel like I can't even muster up the energy to go like I used to when we first got together."

"Bet you're really stressed out about finances, right?"

"Yeah."

"Finances are the one thing that can alter a relationship—if the money is not right, it's hard to get other things right," Deana said. "So...how many times a week? And Alisha, don't play like you're all shy."

Alisha paused, and Deana looked at her.

"Spit it out," Deana said.

"Maybe once or twice a week," Alisha admitted.

"Are you serious?! You're practically a born-again virgin. As for me, it has to be at least five times a week," Deana declared. "Haven't you heard the expression 'if you don't use it, you'll lose it'? You are too young to be collecting cobwebs, girl. The way you're going at it, you leave the door open for somebody else. If I were you and I were married, my man would be calling in to his job saying 'Man down! Man down!', and 'I don't think I'm going to make it'," Deana joked.

"Girl, you are crazy! That is hilarious," Alisha said, and they both laughed together.

"Remember I was telling you about that young guy I was dating a little while ago?"

"Yeah, I remember," Alisha said.

"We were at the shop one night; child, I had him out of breath, pouring down sweat, and begging for water," Deana cracked.

Alisha smirked, then broke out laughing.

"Don't underestimate the power of the Apple pie," Deana said.

"Yeah...but I'm just plain Jane; I want to be spontaneous, but...sometimes I feel like I haven't reached that point with my husband. I don't know if it's all the stuff that I'm going through that stops me from reaching that point, but...it's like I just can't let go of myself," Alisha said.

"So, what you're saying is, he's not loving you right?"

"Well, yeah—and no, to a degree; but what do you think I should do?"

Deana thought for a moment. "Well first off, let me ask you: have you ever felt like you reached that point of satisfaction?"

"Honestly, no," Alisha admitted. "It's like I get to the cliff, but I'm never pushed over the edge."

"Alisha...you have so many things going for you. You're a beautiful young lady with a nice body, a beautiful face...he should be making you happy, whatever it takes."

They continued talking until they arrived back at Alisha's house.

"Are you still coming in and hanging out with me a little while longer?," Alisha asked.

"Yes, I can stay about another hour so," Deana said.

As they entered the house, Alisha called out to Darien.

"Honey, I'm home!," she yelled. Darien, who was in the living room watching TV, yelled back, "I'm back here, baby."

As Deana complimented Alisha on how nice her home looked, Darien walked into the hallway.

"Oh, we have company," he said, surprised. "You must be Deana." He reached out to shake her hand.

"Yes, I am."

"Alisha has told me so much about you."

"Good things, I hope," Deana responded.

"Yeah, it's all good," he said. "You're her newest friend. Come on in and make yourself at home."

"Do you want anything to drink?," Alisha asked.

"No, thank you," Deana said.

"I'll be right back," Alisha said, walking towards the bedroom. Deana sat on the couch and talked to Darien.

"I see the game is on; who's winning?," she asked.

"New York is up by 10," he answered. "So, you're into sports?"

"A little bit. In my line of work, I have to be a jack-of-all-trades."

The game went to a commercial break and Darien continued the conversation with Deana.

"I hear you guys are going to Atlanta," he said.

"Yes, I have some business meetings to go to down there, and I'm trying to hook your wife up with people who could potentially open some doors for her in the future."

"That's good," Darien said.

Alisha came back and sat on the couch.

"He hasn't talked you to death about sports, has he?," she asked Deana.

"No, I'm fine. I like sports too!"

About two hours later, everyone was still laughing and having a good time. Darien was telling them details about some of the reality shows he'd recently watched.

"I want to stay, but I really have to go," Deana said regretfully. "I'm gonna have to catch up with you all some other time. I have to go home and get ready for work tomorrow."

"We hate to see you leave; it's not often that we have this much fun with company," Darien said.

"Yes, I had a good time with you guys tonight—we will get together and do it again sometime soon."

"That sounds great," Alisha said, walking Deana out to her car. "Thanks for everything today; I really thank you for going down to my Mom's with me. It really meant a lot."

"It's all good—I'll call you tomorrow to and see what you've got going."

Alisha waved goodbye as Deana drove off, then walked back into the house.

"What did you think about her?," Alisha asked, curious to know what her husband thought of her new friend.

"She seems nice," Darien said.

"So, you like her better than Lindy?"

"Yes, anybody is better than Lindy," Darien said honestly. "I just think she's a bad influence; she has nothing going for herself, and she just has a bad reputation in the city. Baby, I just don't want you to be caught up in any bad situations with a person who has nothing to lose."

"I hear you, baby—and I understand where you're coming from," Alisha said, trying to measure her words. "I don't want to put myself in bad or compromising situations; but underneath all of Lindy's partying, loudmouth drinking, and all of that, there is a good person," she said, defending her friend, "and to be very honest, she always—and I mean *always*—speaks well of you."

"Well, that's good; I believe there's somebody good underneath her outward persona," Darien agreed, "but she's just got to get *better*."

"Maybe so; but she's still a good person," Alisha said, having the last word about her friend.

Alisha entered the bathroom to take off her makeup. Darien came in and kissed her on the neck.

"I've been missing you all day," he whispered, kissing her again. "Why don't you put on that nightgown that I like?"

"Baby...I'm really tired; it's been an extremely long day, and I'm just not in the mood." As she spoke, she remembered what Deana had said to her in the car; she turned around in his arms.

"Okay," she smiled. "Just a little bit..."

Darien picked Alisha up and brought her to the bedroom. He laid her on her side of the bed, and began to make love to her. It wasn't long before he noticed that she was not into it. He stopped and looked at her.

"What is it?," he asked.

"Nothing," she replied.

"No," he said, sitting up. "There's something wrong."

"It's nothing," she repeated.

Darien got up and walked around to his side of the bed. Alisha sighed. "I told you, nothing is wrong," she insisted.

"Alisha, I can tell something is wrong with you. Did something happen today?"

"No," she said, with a puzzled look on her face, "nothing happened today."

"Then why are you not into it tonight?," he questioned.

"I'm just not into it...I guess I'm just really tired."

"It seems like you're always tired."

"I'm not always tired..."

"Yes, you are; and I totally understand."

Alisha reached over and pulled herself closer to him.

"Baby, don't be like that; I'm just tired... just hold me," she said. Darien put his arms around her.

"I know I have been a little distant lately," Alisha said, "but a lot is racing through my mind."

"We are still newlyweds," Darien pointed out. "We should be all over each other...but it seems as if we're drifting apart."

Alisha held Darien closer. "Just because I don't want to have sex with you every night does not define how much I love you," she told him.

"Yeah, but there should be some sign that you do. Like they say in church, faith without works is dead; well, Marriage without SEX is on life support."

"I wish you could've gone to church with me today," Alisha said. "Pastor Jones was awesome today, it seems like everything he said was directly to me."

"That's good."

"He asked about you. After service, I talked to him about a few issues I was having, and he knew just what to say."

"I lay in bed with you every night," Darien said. "You never talk to me."

"That's not true, I do talk to you...I just needed some spiritual counseling for what I was going through. I'm really serious about us starting back to go to church. I think that's something that we need to do together."

"Baby, we will," Darien assured her.

She kissed him. "I know you have to get up in the morning, so let's go to sleep."

Everything in Darien in Alisha's household ran on at its normal pace until two weeks later, Alisha found herself getting ready for her trip to Atlanta. That morning, she pulled out her suitcases and started filling them with clothes. Darien looked at the stuffed suitcases.

"Do you plan on coming back, or are you running away?," he asked jokingly. Alisha just laughed.

"Got to look good for this event! This could potentially open the door to a lot of other things," she said.

"I see some new stuff with the tags still on it," Darien noted. He took a second look.

"Alisha...these are some very expensive tags on these shoes," he said, puzzled. "And since when did we start buying $300 shoes?"

"I already know what you're thinking," Alisha said, "Deana bought me the shoes."

Darien had a surprised look on his face.

"Oh, really? Alisha, I have to be honest and say I really don't believe that."

"It's true," Alisha insisted. "A couple weeks back, we went to the mall and I was just looking at the shoes; and she paid for them for me."

Alisha's answer only raised more questions in Darien's mind.

"Alisha, why would someone you just met buy you all of these expensive gifts?," he asked. "This is something that another man would do."

"Darien, I told you: Deana bought this stuff," Alisha stated again.

"Right!," Darien said.

"Well, I don't know what else to tell you," Alisha said, not wanting to argue about it. "If you think I'm lying, you can call Deana and ask her yourself."

"Just forget it," Darien said, not wanting an argument either.

"I don't understand why you're getting mad because somebody else did something for me."

"As bad as I hate to say it, Lindy didn't even do stuff like this—and you've been friends with her forever," Darien said. "But you know what? I don't want to spoil your morning. I don't want you to leave on a bad note, so I'm just going to leave the whole matter alone."

Darien walked out of the bedroom. Alisha continued to pack her clothes. She got a text message from Deana that said, *I'll be there at 10 o'clock.*

She replied to the text, *I'll be ready.*

Alisha went into the kitchen and came up behind Darien, wrapping her arms around him.

"Don't play like that; you know you're going to miss me."

He turned around, smiling at her.

"You know I'm going to miss my sweet thang," he said.

"Aww!! My teddy bear is going to miss his sweet thang." She kissed him, and squeezed him tighter.

"I'll be back so soon you won't even know I'm gone," she said. With another kiss, she said, "baby, you're going to be late for work."

"Now, I *can* be late if you want me to," Darien said as he pulled her closer, with that look in his eye.

"No, you go to work," she told him. "I'm going to miss you while I'm gone; I'll call you as soon as I get to the airport, before I board the plane."

"Okay," he said, reluctantly letting his wife go. "I will let you go...I love you, girl."

"I love you too," she said, with a final kiss.

Chapter 4

Going in

As Alisha was finishing packing for the trip to Atlanta, Lindy called.

"What's going on?," Lindy greeted her.

Nothing, just on my way to Atlanta," Alisha said, trying to sound casual.

"Going to Atlanta!," Lindy exclaimed, *"I don't remember you telling me that you're going to Atlanta. You didn't even ask me if I wanted to go there."* Alisha could hear the disappointment in her friend's voice.

"Yes, I did. I told you a little while ago; maybe you just don't remember."

"I don't remember that," Lindy said. *"And I suppose you're going with your new BFF."*

"Lindy, don't start tripping."

"All I'm saying is, this is a woman that you don't know anything about. You are traveling with her, and she's doing all of this weird stuff for you...I think you need to think about it, Alisha."

"Think about what?"

"I've seen this plot in a movie before—how the woman butters you all up, you think she's cool; you bring her to your house, then all of a sudden—BAM!!! You walk in from work one day you catch her and your husband going at it like rabbits."

"Girl, stop! That is not going to happen. No way no how," Alisha said.

"Well," Lindy said dryly, "I'm not going to play the 'jealous friend' type, so I'm just going to say have a good time, and call me when you get there, because I want you to bring me some shoes back."

"You know I wouldn't go all the way to Atlanta and not bring you anything back, girl!"

"Okay," Lindy said, satisfied. "When you get back, we're going to hang out so you can spend some time with your real BFF."

"I'll call you when we get to Atlanta."

"Okay. Take care, be safe."

Alisha got off the phone, and pulled all of her luggage to the front door. She made herself some coffee and had a cup before it was time to leave. Shortly after finishing her coffee, Deana called and said "I'm outside."

"I'll be right out," Alisha said, as she turned off lights and checked doors. Moments later, she came out and put her luggage in the trunk and got in the car.

"Hey, how you are you?," Alisha said.

"Tired. I'm going to sleep like a baby on this flight."

"I hope not, because I haven't all the way gotten over my fear of flying."

"Church Girl, you'd better pray, because I'll be asleep," Deana chuckled.

"What did you do last night?"

Deana made a face. "I went out on a date with someone who is clearly not my type, and not going in my direction," she said. "It seems like I can never find that one thing that makes me happy in anybody. I don't know if I'm just high-maintenance or picky, but I feel like I deserve to be loved right—and I refuse to settle. I'm going to get what I want one way or another."

"I hear you," Alisha agreed, "that's how I was with Darien. When I met Darien, I knew he was the one—no doubt about it, hands down that was my man."

"I hear you on that, girl," Deana laughed.

Right then, she got a phone call from her assistant.

"The next time he calls, get his number," Deana told her assistant. "I'll talk to him myself...I have no problem with cussing him out." She hung up the phone.

"I'm just so tired of people being all in my business. This is my life. I'm tired of people trying to dictate to me what I should and shouldn't do," Deana complained. "I'm free, and just because I don't do things in a conventional method doesn't make me a monster or criminal. Alisha, you just don't know some of the struggles that I go through," she continued. "People look at my car, my house, my job, at the things that I have...the people don't know some of the struggles that I endure on a day-to-day basis. The funny thing about life is, most people think that once you have a lot of money, you are exempt from problems and struggles; but if I could tell the truth, the more money you have, the more struggles, the more problems you have. Alisha, one reason that I like being around you and doing things for you is, you don't expect me to do anything for you. You're not disappointed if I don't do anything for you—and some of the things you say to me just uplift my spirit. I am really happy to have you as a friend, and in all honesty, I felt drawn to you. Maybe it was the whole 'church girl' thing that made me feel safe enough to let my guard down, and let you see certain aspects of my life. Alisha, I've got friends I've known for 10 and 15 years that I've never taken shopping to buy anything; I just want to say that I appreciate your friendship...after all of that, I don't know whether to cry or whether to give you a hug."

Alisha smiled at Deana.

"Aww!! As soon as we get out of the car, I'm giving you a big hug."

"I'm not going to let you make fun of me anymore," Deana said, and they both laughed.

Not too long after standing in line to go through the airport metal detectors, Deana got a call, and answered her phone.

"I'll bet you I can," she said confidently. "You know, I don't take 'no' for an answer. I've put in too much work for this bid."

Deana got off the phone and looked at Alisha, who had overheard Deana's end of the conversation.

"People always underestimate me," she said.

"Me too," Alisha agreed.

About 45 min into the flight, Deana looked over at Alisha, who didn't seem to be doing too well.

"Are you all right? You look kind of jarred...look, I'm not holding your hand; you have to *relax*. Just close your eyes and try to relax...we'll be there in no time."

"Yes, that's easy for you to say—you probably fly all the time."

"Please don't get sick on me."

"I'll be all right," Alisha said weakly.

Deana took out her iPod and handed it to Alisha.

"Here. Just listen to some music."

Alisha took the iPod and slipped on the headphones. She began to calm down, and managed to stay that way for the rest of the flight.

When she got to Atlanta, she called Lindy as promised.

"Girl, I can't believe that I'm in Atlanta," she said. "It's beautiful here."

"Yeah, all of that is nice, but how do the men look there?"

Alisha laughed. "I've seen a few just the way you'd like them," she said.

"Don't make me get on a travel site, find a cheap ticket, and get down there tonight!," Lindy joked.

"Lindy, you would hurt himself. All of these clubs. All of these men...you would go crazy."

"Yep, you're probably right."

Alisha heard a familiar voice in the background.

"Lindy! I know that's not who I think it is," Alisha scolded.

"What are you talking about?," Lindy asked, trying to play clueless.

"You know what I'm talking about—after all of that fussing and crying you did, you've got Tyland back over there."

"You are right," Lindy confessed, trying to keep her voice low. *"I've got it bad; I'm trying my best to leave him alone, but...it seems as if he knows all the right words to say. Then on top of that, he comes right in my house and start taking off his shirt. He stood in front of me shirt open, muscles bulging; I went from En Vogue to Britney Spears!,"* she joked. *"When he first walked in, I was like 'you're never going to get it', then two hours later I was singing 'Oops!! I did it again'..."*

"You are beyond crazy! I'll call you later on, once we get settled and everything."

"Okay. Later."

Moments later they arrived at the Ritz Carlton. Alisha walked through the door into the front lobby.

"Wow, this is a really nice hotel."

"Yes, it's one of the best," Deana said.

She went to the counter and gave the attendant her name; he pulled up the reservations.

"Do you have any suites?," Deana asked.

"Let me check and see what's available," the attendant said. He paused for a brief moment.

"We have one available for you," he said.

"Does it have a whirlpool in it?"

"Yes, it does."

"That's the one I want," Deana smiled. She turned to Alisha.

"Hope you don't mind, but I *have* to be in a whirlpool."

"That's fine with me," Alisha said, "because I would love to get in there myself. I haven't been in a whirlpool since my honeymoon—and my back and feet are killing me."

As they both stand at the counter, Alisha is amazed at the rate of the room. When they entered the room, Alisha was still in amazement.

"This is better than the room I had on my honeymoon," she declared.

"I knew you would like it," Deana said. "I am crazy about the suites here, they are absolutely wonderful."

As they got settled in, Alisha noticed that there was only one bed in the room. *I am not sleeping in the bed with her*, Alisha thought to herself, so she went in and laid her luggage by the couch.

"Want to put your stuff in the closet? You can take the bed tonight, 'cause I always stay up late and watch TV,"

Deana said. "You take to bed tonight, and I'll be on the couch."

"No, that would definitely be wrong on my part," Alisha protested. "I can't take the bed, you paid for the room."

"I'm not worried about all of that, girl. All I need is a laptop and a TV—that's what I'm most concerned about! By the way, I don't have my laptop; do you have yours?"

"Yes," Alisha said.

"Can I use it in a little bit?," Deana asked. "I've gotta check my e-mails to make sure everything is going to be on point for us when we go to the gala tomorrow," she explained. "I've got some friends coming by later on, so we're going to hang out with them; oh, and I am warning you right now—they are kinda crazy."

"I hope not too crazy," Alisha said. "So, what should I wear?"

"Just put on something—you know: classy, sexy, whatever."

"What time will they be here?"

"In about an hour or so, so you have plenty time to change clothes and do what you need to do," Deana said.

Alisha went into the bathroom to check out the whirlpool.

"This thing is huge," Alisha told Deana. "I can't wait to get in here."

"Go ahead and do your thing, then."

Alisha started to unpack some of the things from her luggage.

"I see that you brought those shoes; I wish we wore the same size, because I would love to wear them," Deana said.

"I might wear these tonight," she said, trying the shoes on. "They look so good on my feet."

"You know, you're right—I can't front, they do look good on your feet." Deana walked into the restroom.

"OMG," Alisha gasped, "I almost forgot to call my husband."

"That's right, make sure you call the old ball-and-chain," Deana hollered back into the room. "We don't want you getting into any trouble tonight."

"Yeah, whatever," Alisha mumbled. She picked up the phone to call Darien but got no answer, so she left a voice message:

"Hey baby, I made it to Atlanta. We just checked into our hotel not too long ago, and baby this room is unbelievable...I'm just unpacking my things. I wanted to give you a call to hear your voice. I love you, call me as soon as you get this message."

Deana walked out of the restroom in time to hear the message Alisha left Darien.

"Aww!! That was so sweet, I almost cried," she teased. Moments later, Deana was on the phone with her friends. She got off for a moment to talk to Alisha and let her know their plans.

"They're on the way, so you can go ahead and get dressed first," she said. "Don't forget to leave your laptop out."

Alisha laid her clothes and accessories out on the bed and got in the shower. While Deana was still on the phone talking to her friends and checking her e-mails, she heard Alisha singing in the shower. Alisha stepped out of the shower, dried herself off, and wrapped up in a towel. She came out and started putting her underwear on. Deana came to the door.

"I didn't know that you could sing, too!," she said, impressed.

"No I can't," Alisha said.

"You have a very beautiful voice," Deana insisted.

"Thank you," Alisha said, accepting the compliment as she stood there in idle conversation.

Deana watched Alisha get dressed as she undressed completely in front of her and walked into the bathroom.

"Wait a minute," Alisha said. "Let me get my stuff out of the bathroom, so you can take your shower."

"Your stuff is alright, but if you need to, come get it," Deana shrugged. Alisha felt awkward; Deana stood there completely nude, and Alisha didn't know what to say or do. Deana finally spoke.

"I'm not with all that funny stuff," she stated. "You are a woman. I am a woman. I know this is new for the both of us. I just wanted to make that clear."

"We're good, no problem," Alisha said quickly; but in the back of her head, she was thinking, *Thank God.*

Alisha finished getting dressed; she was about to give Lindy a call while Deana was still in the shower, when she heard Deana's phone start to ring. Deana yelled for Alisha to go ahead and answer it.

"Hello, who's calling?," Alisha asked.

"Hi, Alisha—you came down with Deana, right? Tell her we'll be there to get you all in about 30 minutes."

"Okay, we'll be ready."

She hung up the phone and gave Deana her friend's message.

"That's fine," Deana said. "I need you to go in my phone and pull up a person by the name of Roland; send him a text that says, 'can we make it about 11:30pm'."

"Okay," Alisha said. She sent the text message, and then came back into the room with Deana.

"Looks like somebody has a hot date for tonight," Alisha teased.

"He's not a hot date, girl, he just has some connections that I need," Deana said. "And as long as I flirt, nobody gets hurt. But the minute I give in, that's when he wins—and that will never happen; so that's why I said you can have the bed. You're my excuse to leave abruptly," she explained. "I'll text you later on; you'll call me right back, and that will be my excuse why I have to leave."

Alisha agreed, and they continued to get dressed; soon enough, Deana's friend called up to the room to let her know they were waiting downstairs. On the elevator ride downstairs, Alisha got a text from Darien.

I see you called me. I was at Tommy's house watching the game, he said.

I miss you baby, everything's okay in Atlanta. I'm getting ready to head out with a few of Deana's friends. I'll call you as soon as I get back in, Alisha texted back.

Moments later Alisha and Deana were out for a night on the town. Alisha rode in the backseat, taking in all of the sights and sounds of nighttime Atlanta. Deana turned around to Alisha from the front seat.

"Are you ready for tomorrow? I have a lot riding on you," she said.

"Sure, I'm ready to give it all I've got."

"That's good. You're going to get the opportunity to see some of the models you'll be working with at the gala tonight."

"That's great, I would love to meet them."

As the dynamic foursome enjoyed an unforgettable night on the town, the time drew closer to 11 o'clock. Recalling her 11:30 appointment with Roland, Deana prepared to cut the evening short with her friends.

"Well, all right you guys. I have to get back to the hotel room...I have some business that I need to take care of," she said.

"Oh! I know what that means," one of Deana's friends hinted, smiling slyly.

"I don't know what you're talking about," Deana said.

"You know what type of 'business' goes on at this time of night," Deana's friend said, looking at Alisha. "It looks like somebody will be swinging from the chandelier tonight."

Everyone in the car started laughing.

"Looks like they're on to you," Alisha chuckled.

"You guys need to quit making fun of me," Deana pouted. Lively conversations and laughter continued in the car until they arrive back at the hotel.

"I'll see you guys tomorrow," Deana said as she got out of the car.

"It was a pleasure to meet you all, you guys are so much fun to hang out with," Alisha added.

"We will see you tomorrow," Deana's friend said.

Going up on the elevator, Deana got a call from Roland.

"Are you ready?," he asked anxiously.

"Give me a few minutes and I will be ready," she replied.

"Okay baby...but don't make me wait too long."

As Deana freshened up before her date with Roland, Alisha made sure she understood what Deana wanted.

"Exactly when do you want me to call you?," Alisha asked.

"Just wait to receive a text message from me, and then call," Deana instructed her.

"Okay, I'll wait on you, then."

"Alisha, don't sleep on this," Deana said, a serious tone in her voice.

"I won't," she promised.

Deana walked out of the bedroom and left the suite. Alisha laid on the bed and began to watch TV. Roland met Deana downstairs in the lobby with 12 dozen roses. Delighted, Deana took the armful of roses.

"How thoughtful," she said, giving him a big hug. Roland walked her outside and opened the passenger

Silly Women & Sleepy Men

door of his brand-new Maybach, and took her to his home.

It was 1:30 in the morning; Alisha received a text message that said, *Call! Quick!,* but Alisha was fast asleep. Deana tried to call her, but still there was no answer.

Roland finally dropped Deana off around 3:30 AM. After several failed attempts at trying to get her to stay, he gave up and brought her back to the hotel. Deana walked into the suite. In the bedroom, she turned on the lamp and found Alisha fast asleep. Exhausted, Deana laid down on top of the covers and drifted off to sleep.

At Nine o'clock Alisha woke up, noticing that Deana, still fully dressed, was in bed with her. *Must have been a rough night,* Alisha thought as she sat up on the edge of the bed. She got up and went to the bathroom to wash her face and brush her teeth. By that time, Deana had awakened from the sounds of the running water coming from the bathroom. Alisha looked up, and Deana was standing in the doorway.

"What happened to you?," she said, still groggy. "I needed you last night."

"I'm sorry," Alisha apologized, "I waited up as long as I could. I thought I wasn't that sleepy; then all of a sudden my eyes got heavy and the next thing I knew, it was morning," she explained. "So how did it go?"

Deana exhaled, shaking her head. "I would rather not talk about it," she said, "the more I think about it, it gives me the creeps...so, are you ready to hit the treadmill this morning?"

"No," Alisha said.

"Come on, it will be fun."

"Well...I guess I could go to the exercise room."

"Don't worry, you can go your own pace. And when you have someone to talk to, it makes your workout ten times easier—the day goes by so quick you don't even know it."

Running side-by-side with Alisha, Deana starts to explain to her what happened the night before at Roland's house. As they both got off the treadmill, Deana's thoughts turned to food.

"Now I'm starving. I can't wait to go get something to eat," she said.

"Me too; I haven't had a workout like this since I was in school. Let's go upstairs and get changed, and we can grab some food while we are out shopping," Alisha said. "I shouldn't be hungry after last night. I have to be honest, that was the most expensive meal I have ever eaten! I am so far in the hole with you, I will need to sell blood to pay you back."

"Just stop it, now—it's no problem for a friend," Deana said.

Back in the room, Deana again offered to let Alisha get into the bathroom to take a shower first; Deana needed to send off some e-mails. Alisha agreed, and headed into the bathroom. Alisha entered the warm water and was enjoying the shower, singing softly to herself.

"Ouch!," she said, rubbing her eyes; her relaxing shower was interrupted when she accidentally got soap in her eyes. She tried to rinse all of the soap out, and turned off the water. Stepping out of the shower with her eyes still burning, she kept them tightly closed and reached for a towel on the shelf.

"Here it is," Deana said.

Startled, Alisha opened her eyes to see Deana standing there.

"Say, you scared me! I didn't even know that you were in here."

"I had to come and hear the Songbird...you don't mind, do you?"

"No. It's cool." Alisha took the towel and wrapped it around her body, while Deana took another towel and wrapped it around her head.

"Thank you," Alisha said.

As Alisha stood in the mirror, Deana began to take off her clothes then got in the shower. Alisha looked at Deana as she stepped into the tub.

"Maybe I do need to work out a little bit more," she said, "your stomach is flat. You have tone like a body builder."

"Thank God for my diet plan and my treadmill!," Deana replied.

Alisha's phone began to ring.

"Tell Lindy I stole her best friend," Deana yelled from the shower.

Alisha picked up her phone and saw a number she wasn't familiar with, so she let it go to voicemail. She went back to the bedroom to lay her clothes out on the bed, then into the bathroom to plug up her flat irons, blow dryer, and curlers.

"Are you ready for today?" Deana asked.

"Yes, I'm ready."

Deana got out of the shower, and stood there.

"Aren't you going to return the favor?," she asked Alisha.

Alisha turned around, giving Deana a blank stare.

"I'm just playing," Deana said, and grabbed a towel off the shelf. Drying herself off, she walked out of the bathroom.

"I want you to do something different with my hair today," she told Alisha. They chatted the entire time that Alisha worked on Deana's hair, then they started getting dressed to go out shopping.

"The gala starts around 7 o'clock," Deana reminded Alisha, "so if you need any more products or anything like that, just let me know and I'll make sure you have them before we get there this evening."

"I think I have everything," Alisha said, putting finishing touches on Deana's style. "Okay, look in the mirror and tell me what you think about your hair."

Deana got up and went into the bathroom, and looked in the mirror.

"Girl, I look like I'm 21 all over again," she said, obviously pleased. "It's a sin to be this pretty."

"Yeah Ms. Thing, you look good—now let me get in here and do something to *my* hair. "You got me on the treadmill, sweating out all of my curls...I have that Afro centric hair."

"Oh, I almost forgot to put on my new perfume after I got out of the shower," Deana said, "tell me what you think about this."

Deana went into her bag, took the perfume out, and spritzed some on her neck. "You can smell it better on me," she said, walking up on Alisha.

"That really smells good; where did you get it?"

"I got it on my trip to Paris. I bought so much stuff in Paris that I almost had to take out a second mortgage," Deana joked.

"I believe it," she laughed.

Deana and Alisha stopped at the hotel restaurant to grab a bite to eat before they went out shopping.

Later on at the gala, the models were preparing for their presentation; Alisha pulled out all the stops to make sure that they looked nothing short of spectacular as she styled their hair. The models and staff complimented her on her work. Deana came back to the dressing room just before the start of the event.

"Ten minutes to Showtime," she said. As Alisha finished her last model to walk out on the stage, Deana gave a sigh of relief; Alisha's hairstyles were great, and at the conclusion of the presentation Alisha was given special thanks for her creative hairstyles.

"Alisha, I knew that you would do well," Deana told Alisha later that night. "Everyone was very impressed by your work."

"I was sweating bullets!," Alisha admitted. "I have never been that nervous to do hair, even though I've been doing hair all of my life. The pressure was still on."

"But you pulled it off! It was really good."

Riding back to the hotel, Deana asked Alisha about staying another day in Atlanta.

"That way, we can relax from all this pressure," Deana said, "and we have the opportunity to do a little more shopping and getting out to see a little more of Atlanta."

"No, I've got to get home."

"No, you don't!," Deana insisted.

"I have to get back home, because Darien is getting ready to leave for Chicago," Alisha explained. "He'll be leaving within a few hours after we get back; if I stay, I won't get back to see him off before he leaves."

"You have the rest of your lives to be together," Deana rationalized. "We're having fun, you have a little money in your pocket...that sounds like a recipe for shoe shopping." Alisha's mind was made up. "I really want to, but I've got to get back home," she said.

"Well, if you must get back to the old ball-and-chain, I guess we'll be leaving tomorrow morning."

"Don't let me ruin it for you; if you want to stay, you can stay—but I've got to get back."

"We came together, we can leave together," Deana said.

###

Later on in the early hours of the morning, Deana and Alisha were laying across the bed talking about everything that went on at the gala: who they saw, and who had on what. Deana was ecstatic, because her clients were happy with her presentation of their product. Her phone was flooded with text messages from friends that were at the gala, congratulating her on a good job.

"You really did a good job, Deana—and I thank you for this opportunity."

"It's nothing, girl...just a small favor for friend."

"No, I'm serious, this really means a lot to me."

As they sat side-by-side on the bed Alisha reached over and hugged Deana.

"I've never had a friend like you," Alisha said. "It seems like the more time we spend together, the more you just unlock certain things in my life; I have told you things that I haven't told anybody. I don't have a lot of friends, and I really consider you my best friend."

Deana hugged her back. "You're going to make me cry," she said, trying to control her emotions. "I have never had a true friend either. It seems like people only want me for what I can do for them, but with you I don't feel like that. When I look at you, I see all the potential that you have and I just want to be a part of your success," she continued. "I'm not demanding that you do anything; I just want to be a part of your success. I just want to see you happy by any means...so, are we best friends now?"

"Of course," Alisha said.

"So that means we're staying in Atlanta?"

"Well, I *still* have to get back."

"Well okay...I'll let you get back. I've tried long enough to get you to stay, but I see you've got to get back to your husband—and put on your maid outfit, Hazel!," Deana laughed. "But since he's going out of town, as soon as we get back and you see your honey bun off, maybe we can hang out if my schedule is free."

"That's great; maybe me, you, and Lindy can all hang out once we get back. I feel like I've left my girl out," Alisha said. "I noticed that she has not called or texted me today."

"Yes, I know. She's jealous—she seems to be very protective of you, and it almost makes me want to ask you another question."

"What?," Alisha asked, puzzled.

"No...you don't want to get into all of that."

"No, tell me," Alisha insisted.

"Well, here we go," Deana started. "I noticed how Lindy is about you...I'd really like to ask, has anything happened between you with her?"

"What do you mean?," Alisha demanded.

"Well, you know," Deana said, "have you two ever slept with each other?"

"NO!!!," Alisha said forcefully. "She has *never* approached me like that—and neither is that my flavor of coffee!"

"I was just asking, I didn't mean to rile you," Deana said. "Since we're on the subject, have you ever engaged in a relationship with a woman?"

"No," Alisha answered. "Have you?"

"Well…once."

"For real?"

"Yes, it happened," Deana said. "Actually, it happened a while back."

"How long is 'a while'?"

"About a year and a half—and I already know what you want to ask me; I see the look on your face."

"What look?," Alisha asked.

"The look on your face that wants to know, 'what it is like being with a woman'?"

"I don't know what 'look' you're talking about…but since you brought it up, go ahead."

Deana began to tell Alisha about her first sexual encounter with a woman. As Deana continued to speak, Alisha tried to navigate away from the conversation, but Deana continued on with vivid and detailed descriptions about her encounters.

"I know at some point you've wondered how it would be, or fantasized about yourself," Deana said.

"No," Alisha said.

"Come on Alisha, you haven't thought about it? At least one time? I know that you're a church girl and all of that; but I know that you've at least thought about it—at least one time," Deana probed. "You're like me: my first time, I refused to believe that something like that would actually satisfy me. Then I thought, what could I do afterwards? I would feel so bad if the other person were to tell anybody about it. I felt like I would have to move completely out of the country."

"But…it's not right," Alisha stated.

"Well, define what is 'right'. Is it right to consistently deprive yourself of finding satisfaction in an unconventional way—or a way that's different from the quote—unquote 'word of God'?," Deana questioned. "Now, I'm not saying that I'm going to protest or march for gays and lesbians, all I'm saying is that people have a right to do whatever they want to do—it's a free country."

"Yeah, but it's still not right by God," Alisha insisted, "and that's just the way that I was taught."

"That's tradition," Deana said, "but you've got to live outside of the box."

"So, what are you saying?"

"I am just saying you need to be open to new things—it's the same as you coming down here with me. If you had stayed back home and said 'I can't do it because I have to work or I have to be at home', you would've closed yourself off from experiencing all the things that you've experienced here in Atlanta," Deana explained. "Alisha, you're like my sister. I will do anything for you, and right now I'm going to be really, really honest—since the time I met you, I've been so in love with you."

Alisha's facial expression began to change; she wore a confused look on her face as she reflected back on Lindy's words: *you don't know anything about this woman…*

"I would do anything for you, Alisha," Deana said as she grabbed Alisha's hand. "I'm serious."

"But…I'm married," Alisha said, flabbergasted. "I can't do that!"

"I'm not trying to take you from your husband. All I'm trying to do is to be there for you and for us to spend time together. I want to share everything with you."

"I can't do this," Alisha repeated, as she trembled and the palms of her hands began to sweat.

Deana grabbed her and she pulled away.

"I can't do that, I'm not gay."

"I'm not asking you to be. I'm not asking you to walk around with rainbows on everything, all I'm asking for is for you to let me continue to take care of you and love you the way that you deserve," Deana pleaded. "I wouldn't dare cause you any heartache or pain at home. I just want to let you know that you always have me as a friend; but because I show my true feeling about you, you're probably going to reject me, you're probably going to leave me alone and you'll probably stop talking to me."

"I'm not going to treat you funny or different, no matter what...you're still my friend. You're like a sister to me. I'm really close to you. I'm not going to treat you any different," Alisha reassured Deana, as she sat there holding her head down. Alisha put her hand on her friend's shoulder and pulled her in close for a hug.

"Regardless, nothing is going to change between us," Alisha said.

"Promise me you won't start treating me different," Deana said.

"I promise. Now let's go to bed. I am still sore from the last work out we did, but I want to try it again in the morning," Alisha said, changing the subject.

She looked over at the alarm clock and noticed the time was 2:45a.m. Exhausted, Alisha laid down in the bed and covered herself up. Deana laid on top of the cover and began to send text messages to her friends. Alisha drifted off to sleep with the longing for her husband's affection and the vivid stories of Deana's encounters on her mind.

Later that morning, Alisha was awakened by a gentle brush against her back; she didn't move and didn't open her eyes. *Maybe it's just an accident*, she thought to herself...and then it happened again, followed by a kiss on the shoulder, and a kiss on the neck.

Alisha turned around and looked at Deana.

"Shhh," Deana told Alisha, putting her finger in front of her lips. "This is our secret."

Deana kissed her again on the neck, and Alisha's mind and body were at conflict. Her mind was telling her "no"; but she couldn't move—she was in a state of shock...and Alisha gave in to Deana.

Chapter 5

If walls could talk

Alisha was just about to step into the shower.

"Are you all right?," Deana asked. "How do you feel?"

"I've never felt like this before," Alisha said; but all the while she was thinking, *this is wrong! I can't do this, I'm a married woman; how can I look my husband in the face, knowing what I've done...and I even brought this woman to my house.* So many thoughts flooded her mind as she stood there in the shower. *God...please forgive me for what I just did,* she thought...and at that very moment, Deana pulled the shower curtain back.

"Can I join you?," Deana asked.

"Sure," Alisha said, awkwardly.

There in the shower, guilt overwhelmed Alisha; Deana tried to talk to her, but Alisha just wasn't herself. She still felt confused about what had just happened.

"I know what you're feeling—and it's okay," Deana said. "I will help you through it. What just happened was not to 'turn' you into anything. It was more about satisfying you, so hold your head up...don't be like that. Nothing has changed. We just shared an intimate moment—the only thing about this is, it's *our secret.*"

"I just don't know how to feel right now," Alisha mumbled.

"Just be you," Deana said.

Later on that day, Alisha called Darien.

"Honey I'll be on my way home in a few hours," she told him. "What time are you leaving?"

"We were going to leave for Chicago about one o'clock, so we can be on time for the seminar tonight," he answered.

"I'm coming back to town as fast as I can so I can see you before you leave for Chicago."

"I hope so," Darien said, *"because I want to see you, too...baby, I miss you."*

"I'll call you as soon as we get back in town," she promised. "Oh yeah, baby—try not to leave before I get there."

"Okay," Darien said, and hung up the phone.

As she'd told him she would, Alisha made it back home in just enough time to catch Darien before he left for Chicago. Deana drove up to the house, and as Alisha got out of the car, Deana flirted with her.

"I'll call you later in the week, maybe we can hang out again," she said.

"Okay, give me a call," Alisha said as she made her way to her front door with her luggage.

Deana drove off and Alisha went into the house. Putting her bags down, she went through the house calling Darien's name. In the bedroom, she found Darien in the closet, sorting through his clothes.

"There you are," she said as she came up and grabbed him from behind. "I missed you."

Pleasantly surprised, Darien turned around and kissed his wife.

"I missed you, too," he smiled.

"What time will Tommy be here?"

"He'll be here in about 20 minutes."

"Baby, do you want me to help you pack any of your stuff?"

"Well, I've pretty much got it," Darien said, but you can make me a sandwich before I leave—I'm kind of hungry."

Alisha went into the kitchen and started making the sandwich; within minutes, she got a text message from Deana.

I can't wait till the next time I see you, it said.

Alisha looked at her phone and hesitated for a moment before sending her reply; *I can't wait either. I can't even think straight. You messed me up real bad LOL.*

Alisha stood in the kitchen texting back and forth with Deana until Darien walked in the kitchen after placing his luggage by the front door.

"What happened to the sandwich?," he asked.

"Oh, I'm sorry...I got caught up on the phone, I'm really sorry," Alisha apologized.

"Don't worry about it, we're getting ready to leave now anyway," Darien said. "Tommy just texted me and said he's outside—and you know how impatient he gets."

Alisha grabbed and hugged him.

"Baby, I'm sorry," she said again, "I really don't want you to go...I just got back, and...I miss you." She kissed him.

"I will be back in no time; you won't even miss me."

"Yes I will," she said, "but I guess you'll call me as soon as you get there."

"You know that I'll definitely call you as soon as I get there."

Alisha held him even tighter. "Okay, let's go over the ground rules: no flirting, no girls in your room, or none of that," she said.

"Baby," Darien chuckled, "none of that is going on with us! We are just hanging out together, that's all—and we are going for business."

"It better be 'business-only', because I tell you, I would hate to have to catch a case. You know I don't play, don't make me have to hurt anybody."

Darien laughed. "Girl, none of that is happening. This could be the opportunity that we've been waiting for to be financially free."

He kissed her again and opened the door.

"Goodbye," he said, taking his bags out to the car. Alisha stood at the doorway and waved at Tommy.

"Don't get my husband in any trouble," she warned.

He waved back at her.

"Don't worry, I won't. I'll bring him back in one piece," Tommy teased.

"Tommy...don't make me have to stick you about my husband." They both laughed; Alisha said goodbye and closed the door.

After they picked up Anthony and hit the expressway, Darien and the guys talked about where they'd be going to eat as soon as they got to Chicago. They argued over who has the best soul food in the city, and Anthony started telling Darien and Anthony about some things that were going on with some mutual friends.

Meanwhile, as Deana was at home unpacking from her trip, she received a text from Alisha.

You are incredible!, the text read.

Deana sent a text message back to Alisha: *you haven't seen anything yet. I'll call you in about an hour.*

Once Alisha got settled she called Lindy; she didn't get an answer the first time, but the second time she called, Lindy immediately picked up the phone.

"Hello."

"What are you doing that you can't answer the phone?," Alisha said.

"Girl, stop it. I was in the room and I didn't hear the phone the first time. I should be asking you that question; you have been acting all brand-new with your new BFF."

"That's not true! You're my girl, no matter what."

Lindy had started getting Alisha caught up about things that had happened while she was gone, when Alisha got a call from Deana; she put Lindy on hold and answered the call.

"I'm bored," Deana said, "why don't we go out and shoot some pool?"

"I don't even know how to play pool."

"Well, that's even better—I can teach you."

"What time?," Alisha asked.

"I'll come get you around eight o'clock," Deana said.

"Okay, I'll be ready." Alisha then clicked over and told Lindy, "I'll call you back later on."

"It must be her," Lindy said dryly. "You two are starting to bother me, but go ahead; I'll just talk to you later."

"Okay, 'bye."

Alisha anxiously awaited Deana's arrival to pick her up. While waiting for Deana outside, Alisha saw her neighbor Greg.

"Hey how's it going?," he greeted her.

"Fine," Alisha replied.

"You'll never guess what I'm having today," he said.

"What?"

"Some of my world-famous meatloaf," he said proudly. Thankfully, Deana pulled up just as Greg was asking if Alisha would like to have supper.

"No thanks," Alisha said, getting into Deana's car. "I'm getting ready to go out."

"Tell your friend that's a nice car—if she ever wants to get rid of it, I'm the man she needs to talk to."

"I'll be sure to mention that."

As she got into the car, Deana said, "what's up, baby?" Alisha was somewhat startled; she didn't know how to respond, and cleared her throat nervously.

"Hi" was all Alisha could manage to say. Deana drove off, and they were on their way to the pool hall.

"Why are you so nervous?," Deana asked. "You act as if I'm going to pull the car over and jump on top of you. Just relax; we're just going out, as normal."

"I'm fine," Alisha said, but she was just as nervous on the inside as she appeared to be on the outside. They arrived at the pool hall and stayed there for about two hours.

When they got back to Deana's house, Alisha walked into the house in amazement.

"This is something that you would see in a magazine," Alisha said, clearly impressed. "It's so clean in here, you can literally eat off the floor!"

"I'm somewhat of a neat freak," Deana admitted.

"That's an understatement," Alisha declared, as she glanced at some of the paintings that graced the walls.

"How did you get so many?"

"I collect them at some of the different places where I've traveled—and it's one of my hobbies, I love to paint." Deana walked into the kitchen.

"I'll get us some wine," she offered.

"No, that's okay, I'm not drinking tonight," Alisha said.

"We've got to have a little to celebrate how well you did for the gala in Atlanta," Deana urged.

Deana poured the glasses of wine and brought them to the couch where Alisha was sitting. She turned on the TV and put a movie in the DVD player. While they watched the movie, Darien called Alisha to tell her how the seminar went. She told him that she was at Deana's house watching a movie.

"I am out with the guys," Darien said. "I just wanted to talk to you before you went to bed—but I see you're out with Deana, so I'll leave you alone. Give me a call when you get home, or in the morning."

"Okay, I love you."

"I love you, too...'bye," Darien said, and hung up the phone. Alisha and Deana continue watching the movie. It was 1:45a.m. when the movie ended, and Alisha thought about her busy schedule the next day.

"I have to get ready for work in the morning, and study tomorrow...I think I need to go home," she said.

"It's already late; you might as well stay here till the morning." Deana went back into her bedroom and got out towels and a silk robe.

"Why don't you go ahead and relax yourself tonight? I'll get up in the morning and take you home," she told Alisha.

"Okay," Alisha agreed.

###

Later on that morning, Deana dropped Alisha off at home then prepared herself for work. As Alisha got ready for her long day ahead, she thought to herself, *I can't believe it happened again.* Darien called her as he prepared for his morning seminar class. After their conversation ended, Alisha sat on the couch and contemplated last night's episode. *I'm not gay,* she thought, *I don't understand why I'm doing this;* but she inhaled and caught the scent of Deana's perfume...and the flashbacks began.

###

At the seminar, Tommy introduced Darien to one of the financial advisers, Sharon.

"Glad to have you aboard," she said, firmly shaking his hand.

"Glad to be here," Darien replied.

"Are you impressed?"

"Yes! I'm really interested in the real estate classes," he said.

"Tommy, I hope you all stick around for my presentation," Sharon said.

"We will," Tommy said.

"I've got to go," Sharon said, "but it was nice meeting you, Darien."

She shook his hand again and walked away.

Anthony walked up as Sharon was leaving; he eyed her from head to toe.

"Man! Who was that?," he eagerly asked.

"That's my recruiter, Sharon," Tommy said. "I came into the company under her."

"Well," Anthony said suggestively, "can I go next? I would *love* to be under her—because Mr. Ball-and-Chain over here isn't going to do anything but window shop…I'm trying to get with her *tonight*."

"I can't lie," Tommy said, "she is a Brick,….House!!!"

"I love it when a woman wears pants like that…ooh wee!!!," Anthony said.

"Don't hump the lady's leg man, chill out!," Darien said, "we came here to get up on some money—that's what I'm focused on."

"Well, I'm just sightseeing right now; I know where the real party is at later on—and it's going to be on," Anthony said.

"It's time for the next class. Let's go so we can find some good seats this time," Tommy said

###

After the classes, Darien and his friends ate dinner at a local bar and grill they found two blocks away from the hotel. As they waited on their food, Anthony said, "man, there's a lot of girls in here! Do you see that girl in the blue jeans over there?"

They all turned around to look.

"Wow," Tommy breathed.

"I'm going to get her number before the night is over," Anthony stated.

"You're crazy!," Tommy said, looking at Anthony sideways. "She is out of your league."

"I'm with Tommy on this one," Darien agreed. "She's major league material."

"Well, I'm a home-run hitter—and I'm going to slide in to first base right now," Anthony said confidently.

Anthony got up from the booth, walked over to the lady, and charmingly introduced himself to a table of three ladies out on the town. Before long, Anthony gave the signal for them to join him at the table, but Darien didn't come; he got on the phone and stayed where he was.

Half an hour went by, and Darien was still on the phone—and the guys were still entertaining the ladies over at their table. Tommy comes back to the table where Darien sat.

"Look, I already know," he said to Darien, "just come and talk to them—that's it! I'm not asking you to do anything else. I just don't want to leave you by yourself."

"I'm good," Darien assured him.

"Come on, man," Tommy urged.

"I'll be over in a minute," Darien said, and continued his conversation on the phone.

Moments later the front door of the bar and grill opened, and Sharon walked in. As the waitress led her to her seat, she walked by Darien; and the scent of her perfume caught his attention, along with every other man she passed. Anthony spotted Sharon from across the room.

"That's not the same woman we saw earlier, is it?," Anthony asked.

"Watch out, ball-and-chain!," Tommy joked, "we might be leaving Darien in Chicago."

"If not, you can leave me, because I'm beginning to *love* Chicago," Anthony said.

As Sharon was seated, she waved at Darien; he got off the phone and waved back. Sharon walked over to his table.

"Is this seat taken?," she asked.

"No," he answered, almost at a loss for words.

"Where is everybody else?"

"Across the room," he answered.

"That's a nice wedding band...where's your wife?"

"Thank you. She's back home in Nashville."

"Why didn't you bring her?," Sharon asked.

"I just needed a little time to get away from the everyday, same-old thing. And Tommy dragged me here. I really didn't want to come, but he is so sold out on this company that he refused to let me have any peace."

"We're glad that you came. A lot of people are skeptical at first, but once you see the money, it makes you a believer."

"How long have you been with the company?," Darien asked.

"I've been with the company about three years and I've already been promoted; I was able to trade in my Honda and get the car of my dreams."

"What car is that?"

"A red Corvette," she said. "I was able to do it in a year and a half."

Tommy and Anthony came back to the table and told Darien that they were going outside to walk the ladies out. Darien and Sharon stayed at the table for about another 30 minutes, in conversation about the perks of the company. After Sharon had a few drinks, Darien excused himself momentarily.

"Excuse me, I need to go check on the guys," he said. He got up and went outside, but to his surprise, his friends were gone and so were the girls. He went back inside.

"Well, I guess they're gone," he told Sharon.

"I guess I should go too," she said. "I have to get up in the morning. I have another presentation to do. I can take you back to the hotel If you would like, it will save you the trip back."

"Okay, let me finish my drink."

When Darien finished, he and Sharon left. As Darien got into her car, he said, "I can't believe they left me." While he was speaking, he got a call from Tommy.

"What happened to you guys? You left me," Darien said.

"We just went out with the girls to put some air in their tire," Tommy explained, *"and we didn't know how long you were going to be talking."*

"Well, I'm on my way back to the hotel."

"He's on his way back to the hotel!," Anthony said in the background. *"Looks like Mr. "I didn't come here for all of that" is trying to get an advance on his investment."*

"I'll just meet you guys back at the hotel," Darien said. Tommy said okay, and hung up the phone.

"My head is hurting," Darien said, rubbing his temples. "I know it hasn't been that long since I had a drink."

"Are you alright? To be honest, you really don't look good," Sharon said, concerned.

"I'm okay."

As she pulled in front of the hotel, Sharon took another look at Darien.

"You don't look good," she said. "I think I should help you to your room."

"No, that's okay I got it...I'll be all right," Darien insisted.

As he held his head, Sharon put the car in 'park'.

"It looks like I'm going to have to take over," she said, paying no attention to Darien's protests of being alright. Sharon walked Darien to the door of his room.

"Maybe you should lay down...you're just not looking really good."

"I don't know what it is; my head is like, really hurting," Darien moaned.

"Does your room have a refrigerator?," Sharon asked.

"No." Darien's voice was little more than a whisper.

"I'll go down to my room, grab some Tylenol and some water, and I'll be back. Is that cool with you?"

"Yes."

"I'll be right back."

Darien went into the room, took off his jacket, and laid across the bed. He sent a text message to Alisha:

Help! I am not feeling good.

There was a knock on the door; it was Sharon. He went to open the door and let her in.

"How are you feeling now?," she asked.

"I'm trying to fight this thing...but I don't know what it is." Darien was miserable.

"You just need to lie down and rest, maybe you're tired."

"Maybe you're right."

Sharon handed him the Tylenol and gave him a bottle of water.

"Thank you for helping me out."

"No problem," Sharon said.

"I don't mean to be rude, but...I really need to lie down; my head is hurting really bad."

"It's no problem" she said, "I'm getting ready to leave; I just wanted to make sure that you're alright."

As she turned and walked towards the door, she said, "I'll see you tomorrow at the seminar."

"Hopefully...if I feel like this, I'm not going anywhere."

"You'll be all right," she smiled.

Darien got up off the bed. "I'm thankful for you helping me and giving me a ride back to the hotel."

"I'll check on you in the morning." Sharon reached in her pocket and began rummaging around. She frowned.

"I can't believe it! I must have locked my key in my room," she said. "Can I use your phone? I need to call the front desk and get someone to come upstairs to let me in."

"Okay," Darien said, exhausted. "I'm just going to lie down for a minute..."

Sharon went over to the phone and called, but there was no answer at the front desk. She hung up and said, "I'll call back in a minute."

She turned on the TV.

"My head is hurting," he said softly, "please turn the volume down low."

"Of course," Sharon said apologetically. She sat in the chair, waiting to call the front desk again. Darien laid on the bed and drifted off to sleep.

Chapter 6

Secret agendas

At 11:30 the next morning, Darien was awakened out of his sleep by Tommy knocking on the door. He rose up in the bed and was shocked to see that he was completely naked!

"Just a minute!," he yelled out to Tommy; he got up, put on his boxers, and went to open the door.

"Man! What happened to you guys last night?," Darien asked.

"No—what happened to *you* last night?," Tommy questioned. "You ate with Sharon, you left with Sharon... you disappeared last night—and when we came to your door, we heard a lot of noise in your room."

"Man...I don't remember anything of what happened last night," Darien confessed. "I had one of the most unbelievable headaches ever...all I really remember is walking up to my room, and everything else is almost a blur."

"What did you drink last night?"

"Whatever it was, I am *never* drinking it again in life," Darien vowed. "I'm going to sit this one out; I'll try to catch the later sessions, but right now I need to get myself together."

"Okay, man—I'll just check with you later."

Darien went back in the room, washed his face and made himself some coffee. He called Alisha to talk to her before she went to her first appointment for the day. When he got off the phone with her, he laid back down on the bed and tries to remember what happened the night before.

Later on that night when all the guys went out to have a good time, Darien was still puzzled in the back of his mind about the night before, but managed to focus on having a good time with his friends. The next morning as they prepared to leave, Alisha sent him a text message:

Sorry I did not get back to you last night, I fell asleep at Deana's, but I can't wait for you to come home. I really miss you.

He replied, *we're getting ready to leave any minute...can't wait to see you either.*

He grabbed his bag and met the guys downstairs in the lobby of the hotel. Darien paid the bill for his room and went to get in the car. Tommy and Anthony took care of their rooms as well, and met up with Darien in the car. Anthony looked at him strangely.

"What's wrong with you, man?"

"Nothing. I'm all right."

"Are we doing breakfast, or are we going straight back home?," Anthony asked.

"I really need to get back home because I'm waiting on something to come through for me," Tommy answered. "We'll stop later on, in a couple of hours."

During the ride home, the three friends talked about different things that were going on; Anthony and Tommy mentioned their mutual friend, Marcus, and his plan to purchase more property. Darien rode along in silence, just listening, until Anthony directed a question at him.

"Hey man, what's going on with your wife's friend?," Anthony asked.

"I don't know," Darien responded, "what's she done this time? She's always doing something; I really wish Alisha would just stop hanging around her. I keep telling her she's a bad influence, and she is always doing something crazy...I'm tired of my wife's name being caught up in it all over town."

"So what are you going to do about it?," Anthony asked.

"Man...honestly, I really don't know; the more I tell her to stop hanging around her, the more she keeps handing me excuses—you know: 'she's *my friend, she's always been there for me and I have to be a friend to her'*—you know, all of that stuff," Darien explained. "Quite frankly, I am sick and tired of hearing her name caught up with something Lindy is doing."

"Lindy is not the friend I'm talking about," Anthony said quietly.

Darien paused for minute. "Which friend are you talking about?," he asked, confused.

"I'm talking about Deana," Anthony said, "it's all over town that she is constantly being seen with her."

"Maybe I'm not following...what's wrong with her? What she do?"

Anthony looked at Darien in amazement. "You seriously don't know..."

Silly Women & Sleepy Men

"No. I don't know," Darien said. Anthony exhaled slowly, then told Darien what he'd heard.

"She is openly gay," Anthony said, "and the word out on the street is your wife is her new woman. And I heard that she spends top dollar for what she wants; but do you want to know the strange thing about it?"

"What?," Darien said, barely able to take in what Anthony was telling him.

"She only goes after married women. She spoils them with all types of expensive gifts to win them over," Anthony said. "Then all of a sudden, she makes her move, and they never see it coming."

Anthony gave Darien a sympathetic look. "Hey, man—I hate to be the one to tell you this...but you're my brother, and I hate for you to be in the dark about what's going on."

A million thoughts swirled around in Darien's head. "Man...I'm speechless. I really don't have anything to say. But when I get home I'm going to deal with this...I can't have that!"

As Anthony told Darien more about Deana, Tommy tried to intervene by changing the subject.

"Man, you just need to talk to your wife," Tommy advised.

"If you don't believe anything I told you, you can ask Marcus," Anthony countered. "He said he saw them in the mall a few weeks ago."

"Man, just leave it alone," Tommy insisted.

Darien stared out the window, trying to control his fury. He sent Alisha an urgent text message: *You need to be at home when I get there. We need to talk!*

###

Back at the beauty shop Alisha chatted with a few of her clients, telling them about how her trip to Atlanta was and all the things she'd seen while she was out of town. She glanced at her phone; the message indicator said she had three messages. She grabbed her cell phone and checked her messages as she walked back to the shop's storage room for more supplies. Deana had sent a text message that said, *I've been thinking about you.*

Alisha replied, texting *same here.*

She saw Darien's message, but barely glanced over it. Grabbing the supplies from the store room, she went back up to the front of the beauty shop. When Alisha got there, Lindy had just walked in the door and the two of them began to talk about everything Alisha had missed while she was away.

###

Later on that evening Darien made it home from his trip. As he got out the car he stopped at the mailbox; *this girl hasn't even checked the mail,* he said to himself. He got the mail out and went into the house. On his way in, he sent Alicia another text message: *Where are you? We need to talk,* it said.

I'm on my way. It'll take about 30 min. before I am done at the beauty shop, she replied. Darien walked in the house, put the bills on the table, and brought his luggage to the bedroom. He came back out to the kitchen and went in the refrigerator to grab something to eat. Darien sat down at the table; as he looked over the bills, he got text message from Tommy: *Thanks for helping me win that bet—I told Anthony that you were going to go to Chicago with us.*

An hour later Alisha came into the house; Darien was sitting on the couch watching TV. She came up to him, saying, "baby I missed you." She sat on the couch next to Darien and kissed him, but didn't get the warm welcome she expected.

"Don't kiss me," he said coldly, pulling away from her.

"Why? What's wrong with you?," Alisha asked, confused.

"So, when were you going to tell me?," he demanded.

"Tell you what?," Alisha said.

"Don't sit here and act dumb," he said angrily, "you know exactly what I'm talking about!"

"No I don't," she insisted, "I don't know what you're talking about! Why do you have this attitude with me?" Darien hastily got up from the couch and spun around to face his wife. He was furious.

"Alisha, how could you sit here and disrespect me to my face?—as if I don't know..." He stopped speaking, taking a moment to gain control of his anger.

"Well, act like it's a rhetorical question," Darien said, his words cold and precise. "Answer me as if I already *know* what's going on with you and Deana."

Alisha got up from the couch; guilt and fear raced through her mind as she realized someone must have spoken to her husband; she had to say something.

"She's just my friend; nothing is going on with me," she lied.

"People are saying she's gay; so, what—now you're gay too?"

"Her sexual preference has nothing to do with my friendship with her," Alisha insisted. "There's nothing going on...where are you getting all of this information?"

"It's all over town that she's gay; it's all over town that she's wining and dining you...it is all over town that you're with this woman—and I can't take it!," Darien thundered. "You have to cut off your connection with her." Alisha's mind was in turmoil; *who's been talking to him?*, she wondered, *and what can I say to make him believe me?!*

"Baby...we're just friends. There's nothing going on," she repeated. "Why are you like this? If you thought I was doing something with her, why would I even allow her to come our house?," she reasoned. "I think you need to stop listening to some of those people that you're listening to—and furthermore, I'm a grown woman. You can't tell me who I can go out with," she said.

Maybe if she acted as though his words insulted her, the story she gave him might sound more truthful; but Darien was not buying it.

"Ohh! So, you're going to do it anyway, after I told you I don't want you hanging out with her," he said.

"I am a grown woman!"

"I guess you're 'independent'; you don't need to run anything by me, nor does anything I say hold any weight with you," he said sarcastically. "Alisha, why has she been buying you all of these gifts?"

"We're just friends—that's it and that's all. Are you doing this to justify something you did in Chicago?," Alisha asked, trying to turn the tables.

"I didn't do anything in Chicago, but obviously you've been busy while I've been gone," he insinuated.

He pauses for a second, giving Alisha a hard look. "You know, I don't have any evidence to prove it...but something is just not right here."

He turned around and walked down the hallway to the bedroom. Alisha walked behind him, still talking.

"So, you're going to let your friends turn you against me and interrogate me over something I wouldn't do?"

"Alisha, just forget it," he said. By his own admission, he had no proof other than hearsay; and he'd long ago gotten used to Alisha winning all their arguments.

Alisha walked up to him and hugged him.

"Baby I love you, you're the only man for me...and if it makes you feel better, I'm even willing to go to the extent of not hanging out with her so much."

"I would prefer that you don't hang out with her at all," Darien said firmly. "Baby...there are just too many things surrounding her name, and I just think she's bad for you."

"Well Darien, you met her yourself," Alisha reminded him, "so you already know how she is; did you get that vibe from her when she came to our house?"

Darien avoided her question, knowing that this was yet another disagreement where she would probably come out on top. "Alisha, just stop it! I don't even want to talk about this anymore...I'm going to bed."

Darien took off his clothes and got in the bed; Alisha went back into the living room. She opened her schoolbooks and began to do a little studying. About an hour later she got a text message from Deana:

Is everything all right?

Yes, everything's all right, why do you ask?, Alisha replied.

I don't know I just know I just felt like something was wrong.

Well, some people have been talking to my husband about you.

What about me?, Deana asked.

They've been telling him that you are wining and dining me and trying to seduce me.

Who was saying that?

Just some people he knows that know you. You know how living in this city is—everybody knows everybody.

Well, there is nothing I can do about that. I am what I am, and I do what I do, I make no apologies for being me, Deana texted. *Alisha, in all honesty I hope that you don't start treating me as if I am not a human being. I am not trying to force you to do anything and I'm not trying to come between you and your husband. All I'm asking for is your friendship. I can't erase what happened between us and if it happens again, so be it.*

Alisha replied, *I am okay with us being friends, but I need to clear my head on all the other stuff we have done.* As she hit the 'send' button on her cell phone, she looked up and saw Darien standing there.

"You must be up texting your lover," he said, eyeing her suspiciously.

"You see, I have my books out—I was using the calculator on my phone! Would you stop being so insecure?," Alisha pleaded.

Darien went to the kitchen. He got a glass out and poured some juice from the refrigerator before going back to bed. When the coast was clear, Alisha sent Deana another text message:

I'll talk to you tomorrow.

Okay, call me after 1:00, after I get out of my meeting, Deana replied.

An hour and a half later, Alisha was yawning and stretching as she read her school material; she laid across the couch with the books and, as usual, drifted off to sleep.

Later on the next morning, Darien came into the living room, fully dressed and ready for work.

"I'm leaving," he said matter-of-factly as he opened the front door to go. Still groggy, Alisha raised herself up from the couch and saw his back as he was leaving.

"So *that's* the way that you leave now?," she asked in disbelief.

"Well, 'bye then! Unbelievable!"

She laid back on the couch.

###

Silly Women & Sleepy Men

Driving to work, Darien heard a commercial that reminded him of Friday's date, October 28th. He thought to himself, *I have to call and make some bill payments.* He felt around in his pockets to make sure he had his check book. Arriving at work, Darien noticed that he didn't see Tommy's car in the parking lot. He walked in and said hello to all of his coworkers and friends. He sent Tommy a text message that said, **where are you?**

Twenty minutes went by, and there was still no answer from Tommy. Darien started working; he again looked at his phone and saw that Tommy still hadn't texted back. He frowned; *this is highly unlike him*, Darien thought, *to miss work and not even call in.*

Later on that day, Darien called Anthony.

"Have you seen Tommy?," Darien asked.

"No, I haven't seen him or heard from him either," Anthony said. "That's kinda weird, isn't it?"

"Yeah, because I always hear from him—and he never misses work."

"That's crazy," Anthony said, "but if I hear from him, I'll tell him that you're looking for him."

Later on as Darien left work for the day, his thoughts were on taking care of business; *I can go ahead and get some money out of the bank and pay the cable bill before they close,* he thought. He arrived at the bank right in the nick of time, with ten minutes to spare. He went up to a teller.

"Hello, how are you?," Darien said.

"Fine, sir—how can I help you?," the teller asked.

Silly Women & Sleepy Men

"I would like to make a withdrawal of $150," Darien told him, glancing at the time.

"Sure," the teller said, "let me see your photo ID and bank card with your accountant information."

Darien got both of them out of his wallet and handed them to the teller.

"I see you have two separate accounts; which account would you like to draw from?"

"Please take it from the joint account."

After a few moments, the bank teller looks at Darien.

"Sorry sir," he said, "the account is overdrawn."

"What do you mean, it's overdrawn?," Darien asked, a confused look on his face.

"A large amount was withdrawn from your account, sir," the teller explained. "That basically wiped out this account."

"When did it happen?!," Darien demanded.

"It happened two days ago, sir," the teller said quietly. Darien was in shock. "Two days ago? I never used my card..."

"Once in the last two days I see a small withdrawal for $200. About five days after that, I see purchases that came through in Chicago, Illinois. Then after that, there was a withdrawal for $11,960," the teller tried to explain, looking at Darien's banking records.

Darien stood there in disbelief; he was completely floored. Everything that he had saved up over the last four years had been taken—and he was left with nothing!

Walking out of the bank, Darien was beyond frustrated as he paced around his truck. He immediately called Alisha.

"Why did you do that?," he shouted as soon as Alisha answered the phone.

"Calm down!," Alisha said, "what you talking about?"

"Alisha! I'm at the bank now, and all our money is gone," Darien said desperately.

"What do you mean, all of our money is gone?!"

"Everything is gone! I can't believe it, everything is gone!"

"Where is your bank card? When was the last time you used it?," Alisha asked.

"The last time I used my bank card, I bought something to eat in Chicago; before that, I only made a withdrawal of $200," Darien explained.

"Well, baby, do you think somebody has used your bank card from one of the places where you made a purchase?"

"Alisha, I just don't know. I just can't think straight right now...I'm on my way home, I'll talk to you when I get there."

"Darien, make sure you calm down. I know how you are when you get overworked."

"Alisha I really can't calm down right now, we have bills with no money, how do you expect me to calm down?"

"Baby, we'll figure it out," Alisha reassured him.

"I'll just see you when I get there," Darien said, and hung up the phone.

Silly Women & Sleepy Men

While driving home Darien started thinking about all of the places where he'd used his bank card in the last week. He got more and more frustrated, because he couldn't think of where the robbery could've happened or even how such a thing could happen. Finally he arrived home, and Alisha came out to his truck. As he got out, Alisha embraced him. "Baby, we're going to figure this out, one way or another," she said, trying to reassure her husband. "The first thing that we need to do is file a police report. I've been on the Internet since you told me about it, and I found out where the withdrawal was made," Alisha told Darien. "Our bank just opened up a new branch on the outskirts of town. It'd take us about 30 minutes to get there from here. The branch does not open on Saturday; we'll have to be there first thing Monday morning."

"Okay," Darien said in a weary voice. "Let's go ahead and get the police involved in this. I want my money back."

As Darien walked towards the doorway, their neighbor Greg waved at Darien and said hello, but Darien didn't look up; he walked straight into the house.

"What's wrong with him?," Greg called out to Alisha.

"I'd rather not talk about it right now, this is not a good time," Alisha said hurriedly, and walked into the house a few steps behind Darien. Alisha was alarmed to see Darien walk out of the bedroom with his gun in his hand.

"I want my money back! Somebody has my money, and I want it back!," he yelled. "I work too hard to let somebody take everything I work for."

"Darien, calm down," Alisha insisted. "We've got to think levelheaded and clear minded at this time." She grabbed the telephone and called the police.

Darien got on the phone and explained to the police what had happened. The officer advised Darien to retrace his steps. After Darien hung up from talking to the police, he called Anthony and told him what happened.

"Man, I *know* you don't think that I would do something like that to you!," Anthony exclaimed. "Man! We've been friends since junior high, and there's no way that I would do something like that. Darien, how much did you lose?"

"Close to $12,000," Darien said, sounding devastated.

"Man...if there's anything that I can do I'll be more than glad to do it; you know I don't have a lot, but whatever I can do, don't hesitate to ask me," Anthony said sincerely.

"Okay, man...I've got to make some more calls," Darien said. "I'll call you later."

"Do you remember dropping your wallet, or leaving your information out, or something like that?," Alisha asked.

Darien thought for a few moments, but came up blank.

"No...I don't remember dropping my wallet or anything like that—or leaving my information out where somebody can see it, I never do that."

"According to the information that I pulled up on the Internet about our accounts, this happened the day you got back from Chicago, baby," Alisha told him. "I hate to say it, but...there's a possibility Anthony or Tommy had something to do with it. You already know how Anthony is. I'm not accusing him, but you already know, he is not the most honest person in the world. And to be honest, I've never trusted him. He's always in and out of jail. He's always involved with some illegal activity that's just not trustworthy."

Darien sighed, feeling frustrated and powerless. "Baby, I'm just not really sure right now; I don't know *who* it is." He went and grabbed his truck keys, heading for the door.

"I'll be back," he said. "I'm just going for a ride to clear my head."

Later on riding through the city, Darien picked up his phone and called Tommy; but once again there was no answer. Alisha called Darien on his cell phone and asked if he was alright.

"I'm fine. I'm on my way home," Darien said. Alisha knew from his tone of voice that Darien wasn't fine. She stayed on the phone with him until he made it back home. When he walked through the door, Alisha came up gave him a reassuring hug.

"We're going to get through this," she said. "Don't worry about it, God will take care of us."

"Well, I need Him to step in right now, because I don't know what to do...that was all of our savings."

"He will baby, you just have to trust Him."

"All I know is, something has to give," Darien said, feeling the weight of the world on his shoulders.

On Monday morning, Darien walked out of the bank and got into his truck. He went into his wallet and pulled out a card with Sharon's e-mail and phone number on it from the seminar he attended. He called the number on the card, and just as he'd suspected, the number was no longer in service. Then, it all became clear to Darien what had happened. The reason why Tommy and Sharon were working together all the time was because it had been Tommy's job to get him to Chicago, and Sharon's job to get his information...it all made so much sense now.

Later on that day, Darien sat down with Alisha and talked about what had happened in Chicago.

Solemn-faced, Darien sat on the couch to talk with Alisha.

"Baby, there is something that we need to talk about," he said.

"What is it?," Alisha asked anxiously.

"While we were in Chicago, Tommy introduced me to a woman who he was affiliated with for the company; she was posing as a sales rep. They were trying to get me to sign up with the company too; but now I've put it all together," he said, unable to hide the anger and betrayal he felt. "Both of them were working to scam me."

"How is that?," Alisha asked.

"Tommy really pressed me to go up to Chicago with him, and now all of a sudden, Tommy is not answering his phone—and has not showed up to work."

"I can't believe that Tommy would do something like that!," Alisha said, shaking her head in disbelief. "He doesn't even seem like that type of person…he's been around us a long time. Tell me, how does this woman come into the picture?"

Darien exhaled slowly, not looking forward to telling his wife how he believed he'd been set up.

"Tommy introduced me to her that night after the seminar," he began. "We were all sitting at the table, and while Anthony and Tommy were off trying to chase women, I sat alone. She came in and asked to sit down at the table with me, and began to talk to me about the business."

"Did you even tell her you were married?," Alisha asked, a note of accusation in her voice.

"Yes! I told her I was married," Darien protested. "I told you I wasn't going there to chase women—I was going for a getaway. Alisha, don't get caught up in that, just hear me out. I'm trying to tell you where all our money went!"

He took a few moments to calm himself before continuing.

"I remember stepping away from the table for a moment and then coming back," he recalled. "A little while after that, I began to get a migraine headache like I've never had before. Normally I never have headaches, you know that; I believe she put something in my drink. Later on that night I was in the room by myself, and there was a knock at the door; it was her, saying she had locked her key in the room and she asked to use the phone."

Alisha had a skeptical look on her face; she looked her husband directly in the eyes.

"So Darien, you're trying to tell me she was in your room, using your phone...and you all did nothing."

"Yes, that's *exactly* what I'm saying," Darien stated. "My head was hurting so much I could barely concentrate."

"Darien, I don't believe that! It sounds to me like you were cheating, and you got what you deserved."

"You're always talking about me telling you the truth, and when I tell you the truth you don't believe it," Darien said, disgustedly. "Alisha, that's what happened—crazy as it sounds, stupid as it sounds—that's what happened. They ripped me off! And that's the bottom line."

Later on that night as Alisha laid in bed, she received a text message from Deana:

Just thinking about you, call me when you get a chance.

As soon as he goes to sleep I'm going to call you, Alisha replied.

"Who was that?," Darien asked when he saw Alisha placing her phone back on the nightstand.

"That was just one my girls checking on me," she said.

"Alisha, I don't want our business all over town."

"And it's not going to be," she replied. "I want you to know that I feel the same way you do—I had money in the account as well. It might not have been as much as you had in the account, but I feel the loss too."

She held him closer and kissed Darien on his back. Moments later he drifted off to sleep. Alisha gently eased out of the bed and went into the living room; she took her phone and turned down the volume to call Deana. As the phone rang, Alisha looked around the corner to see if Darien had noticed that she was out of the bed; the coast was clear. She sat on the couch and told Deana the whole story.

"Girl, and you believe that?," Deana asked.

"Yes, I believe him...I think he's sincere," she answered. Deana wasn't convinced. "You're in a hotel room with another woman, and nothing happened; you wake up, and you're bankrupt...that sounds a little fishy to me," she said, not even trying to hide her suspicion. "Men will be men, and there's no possible way you will ever get me to believe that they were in a hotel and nothing happened! It's very difficult to digest something like that...Alisha, I know that's your husband, and you love him, but look at the facts."

"I'm not sure...I really don't know what to believe; I'm trying to support him because I know how hard he has worked to try to provide a better life for us—contradictory as that might sound. I believe in him one hundred percent...and at the same time, I don't believe he didn't sleep with that woman."

"Well, you have to go with your heart and where it leads you, because the bottom line is the money is gone—and at the end of the day, you are left financially devastated."

"I know that's right," Alisha sighed, "we really don't know what to do. We've gotten the police involved, and our lives have literally come to a standstill because of this; we can't sustain this house and all our other bills with nothing. It is very hard to deal with the situation and keep the idea that it's not his fault—that he actually didn't do anything wrong...it is very difficult for me to believe that."

"All I'm saying is, if your heart is saying that something is not right, follow your heart. Alisha, anyway this goes, I want you to know that I have your back—if you need anything, let me know."

"Okay. Thanks."

"Well, I have some things I've got to do early in the morning, so maybe we can do lunch—that is, if you're not busy. What time are you going to the shop?"

"I don't have a lot of clients tomorrow, so I won't be at the shop until around 1:30."

"Great," Deana said, "we can do lunch around noon at the café in the mall."

"Okay. I'm getting ready to go and lay back down before he notices I'm gone," Alisha said, "I'll just call you in the morning."

Alisha hung up the phone, went back to the bedroom, and laid very gently in the bed with Darien still fast asleep.

###

After everything that had happened, it was inevitable; the next day, Darien woke up feeling really low. The more he thought about the whole situation, the more depressed he became, and still there were no results from the police department. Darien walked around his job in a daze, as if the weight of the world was on his shoulders...and there was nothing he could do about it.

The word soon got around the office about what had happened to him, and Darien's co-workers began to look at him with pity. He just hung his head, not making eye contact with anyone; it was all he could do to just continue on with his day.

Later on that day, Alisha met Deana for lunch. Deana signaled for the waitress and ordered her usual meal, but Alisha had no appetite.

"I'm not really hungry," Alisha said. Deana just looked at her.

"I know you're going through some things," Deana said gently, "but come on, eat something—you'll feel better."

"No, I really don't want anything, I just want to sit here and talk, basically." Alisha looked up at the waitress and said, "just bring me some water with lemon—that'll be all, thank you."

"Wait just one second before you walk away from the table," Deana instructed the waitress, "go ahead and get her some of that chicken noodle soup."

"That's great, you're really going to love it," the waitress replied, "that's one of our specialties—everybody loves it." As the waitress walked away, Deana turned to Alisha.

"Alisha, I can't stand to see you like this," Deana said. "I've got to do something...you've got to go out, you've got to get your mind off what's going on! You've got to get free from this. I know it's a difficult situation to go through, but I want you to know again: I'm always here for you...if you need something, I won't let you go without."

"I'm no lawyer, and I have no idea what legal course we can take to get our money back...it's just so difficult to deal with this whole thing with Darien."

"I can't take it anymore! I'm taking you out tonight—I'm making an executive decision here, it's not up for debate. We're going to go out, and that's a done deal," Deana said. "Not only that, I'm going to take you somewhere as soon as we get through eating."

"Where are we going?"

"The only place that would make a girl feel better in a time like this."

"Where is that?," Alisha asked.

"We're going back to that shoe store in the mall, because nothing makes a girl walk with her head up like a new pair of heels," Deana declared, "and Alisha, *don't* look over here and tell me you don't have any money...don't start acting brand-new, you know I got you."

Later on that evening Alisha called home and talked to Darien.

"I'm going to go out with some friends, just to clear my head...I'll be home a little later. I'll see when I get in."

"Alisha, who are you going out with?," Darien asked.

"You know...Lindy," she stammered.

"No, you're not going out with her, I know it—I can tell the way you say it; it's in your voice."

"Darien why are you acting like this?," Alisha said, getting defensive. "I told you what I'm getting ready to do, why are you trying to make it more than what it is? I'm going through it just like you are, this affected me just like it affected you, so please let me go out and clear my head—just for a minute."

"Okay," Darien snapped, "I'll let you go—'bye!" and hung up abruptly.

Alisha looked at the phone, saying to Deana, "I'm not even calling him back...I don't feel like arguing or fighting."

"You shouldn't have to! This is girls' night out, and I'm going to cheer you up one way or another."

Deana took Alisha out to a nice bar and grill owned by one of her acquaintances. A few hours and drinks later, Alisha was intoxicated.

"It's time for us to go," Deana said, noticing Alisha's sleepy look.

"Yes, because my head is spinning now," Alisha slurred, "and I've got to get home—it's almost 12 o'clock."

"Okay; I'm taking you home now."

When they got in the car and hit the expressway, Alisha was awake and talking to Deana; soon enough, the liquor took its toll and she dozed off to sleep. When the lights came on in Deana's car, Alisha woke up to find that she was at Deana's house.

"Deana, I thought you were taking me home," Alisha said groggily.

"I just needed to stop and do something, because I'm not staying at home tonight," Deana explained. "I'm staying on your side of town. You can stay in the car or come in with me; I won't be long, I promise."

"Okay, I can come in for a second...but I've got to get home."

Alisha made her way inside and sat on the couch. Deana headed back into her bedroom, saying, "I'll be right out in a second."

About 15 minutes went by; finally Alisha yelled back to Deana's bedroom to see what was going on.

"Are you all right?," she asked. "Do you need me to help you do something?" She'd waited long enough, and was trying to rush Deana out the house.

"You know what? Actually, I do need you...could you come back here for a second?"

Not knowing what to expect, Alisha got up and walked back to the bedroom, but the door was closed; she knocked on the door.

"Come in," Dean said. Alisha opened the door and to her surprise, there were candles all over the room...and before she could take her next breath, Deana grabbed her...and took her by surprise.

Silly Women & Sleepy Men

Alisha walked through the dark silent house; she stopped at the bedroom door and listened to see if Darien was sleep. Satisfied that Darien was fast asleep, Alisha took off her clothing and rushed into the shower. The alarm clock she passed said 1:45a.m. She got into the shower; *I am so confused*, she thought to herself. Minutes later, she managed to ease into bed without waking Darien up. As she closed her eyes, Darien turned over, staring at her in the darkness.

"Why don't you just divorce me and be with her?," he asked, a defeated tone in his voice.

"Darien...what are you talking about? Because I took a bath, that means I did something? I told you, I'm not like that," Alisha said; but her words lacked truth.

"Alisha, stop!!," Darien demanded. "You're in denial. I can tell something's going on...be honest with yourself, you know this is not right." Darien sat up in bed. "Alisha, it's 2 o'clock in the morning—you don't even stay out that late with Lindy," he said. "Oh, yeah—and I know that you weren't with Lindy, so don't try to use that excuse...after all that we're going through together, you just up and decide to do something like this."

"Darien, I told you I just needed to go out and clear my head—that's all."

"Don't you think that's something that we should work on together, instead of you trying to see someone in secret—someone that you know is after you?," Darien demanded. "And furthermore, it's a dead giveaway—you just came in here and took a bath at 1:45 in the morning, Alisha! Stop!"

"Darien, the only reason why I did that was because I wanted to have sex with you...but obviously that's not going to happen now. I'm really tired, and I don't feel like dealing with all this drama tonight."

Alisha got out of bed and went to the living room; she laid on the couch, contemplating what she should do.

For the next few weeks, Darien and Alisha's relationship took a 180 degree turn as they began to face the harsh realities of identity theft and a breakdown in their communication. Finally, it happened: Alisha and Darien got into an argument that was so bad they called it quits afterwards, and they went their separate ways. Alisha moved in with Lindy, while Darien kept the house until he found a buyer. Two months passed by with minimal conversation between Alisha and Darien.

Chapter 7

No Regrets

One night, Lindy and Alisha were sitting up having a girls' night watching Lindy's favorite movie on TV with popcorn and candy.

"So...when are you going to get your man back?," Lindy asked casually.

"I'm fine without him," Alisha said. "In all honesty, it looks like we're heading towards divorce court; we're just not seeing eye-to-eye anymore."

"As long as you all have been together? Girl, you all came up from nothing; I remember both of you, when you were struggling...and you loved each other." Lindy looked at Alisha, shaking her head sadly. "All I'm saying is, girl you have changed in the last couple of months."

"What do you mean?," Alisha questioned. "I'm still the same person."

"No; something is going on, and all I'm saying is, you might want to stop and think for a minute before you throw this whole marriage away over some disagreements," Lindy advised. "Let's just be honest, Alisha—there's not a lot of good men out here like Darien. You can play this 'independent' stuff all you want to, but I know the real you. I know how you really are, and you two need each other. You two are made for each other."

"Yeah, what if I already have somebody who's willing to love me?"

"If you're talking about love already and you guys just broke up, obviously it tells me you've been doing some creeping—and you haven't told me any of the juicy details," Lindy said, summing up the situation.
She paused for a second, then realization hit her.

"Wait! It all makes sense now," Lindy said, looking at Alisha. "I know this is none of my business, but...I want to know. Alisha...are you messing around with Deana?"

Silly Women & Sleepy Men

Silence filled the room as Alisha took a handful of popcorn and put it in her mouth; she could not look at Lindy. Lindy got up off the couch and stood there, looking at her friend. She sighed.

"I kind of suspected that, but I didn't want to believe it," she said.

"Don't start judging me, Lindy," Alisha said defensively. "I love my life—this is my life, and I can do whatever I want to do. I'm in love; and this is better for me; there's no more financial struggles...when I'm with her, I feel like the sky is the limit."

"You can't be serious, Alisha! You're a Church girl! And if that wasn't bad enough, you haven't even been married a whole year yet. Does Darien know about it?"

"Well, I think he does now," Alisha admitted. "And it doesn't matter, because he doesn't really care about me—his idea of loving me is paying bills and having sex. He doesn't even talk to me, or understand some of the things that I'm going through," she rationalized.

"He's a man! No, he's _not_ going to understand what a woman's going through—that's why _you've_ got to be up front with him, and be open," Lindy stressed. "I have dated enough married men to know what all of their complaints are about; the reason why they don't really talk to their wives is, sometimes we as women give them too much extra information, and they don't really know where to start trying to solve the problem," she explained. "But if we were to start being upfront and honest, and deal with the main breakdowns in our lives, then the man can do what men do best: that is, fix stuff."

"What do you mean fix stuff?"

"Girl, Men are simple! Most of them love to fix something. They were taught this as children—to take something broken that a woman gave him, bring it back to her, and say Look! I fixed it."

Alisha had to laugh at Lindy's assessment of men. "Girl, you're crazy! Where did you get that from?"

"Tell me if I'm right," Lindy said. "After you started getting all of those expensive gifts, he started getting suspicious."

"Yes, you could say that," Alisha agreed.

"Then after that, probably what happened is you began to be distracted during sex."

"Well...I guess you could say that too; it just wasn't the same for me."

"Alisha, you know why," Lindy stated.

"Why?," Alisha asked.

"When you started receiving those gifts and your attention was going elsewhere, it probably made him feel useless and unappreciated. See, you have to understand: a man's ego is built on what he can do; when there is nothing for him to fix, in most cases he feels like you don't appreciate him. The reality is that a man would do anything for a woman's approval," Lindy continued. "Girl, if your mentality about your sex life has gotten down to the 'hurry-up-and-get-through' level, you're not making him feel like he's the man...you have now basically put the nail in the coffin."

Alisha could hear a lot of truth in what Lindy was saying, but didn't want to admit it. "How do you know all this stuff is right anyway?," she asked.

"Like I said," Lindy repeated, "I've been with enough married men to know why they all talk about their wives—and if she would do just this one thing, they would be happy."

"If you know all of this and all of this is right, why haven't *you* gotten married yet?"

"There's just too many to choose from, girl, and I can't have just one," Lindy joked.

They both began to laugh as Lindy sat back on the couch.

"Alisha, I think you making a very big mistake," Lindy said, all joking aside. "I think this woman came into your life and lured you away to give up your house and your marriage. Just because something is new doesn't necessarily make it right...you are a married woman; you took vows before God. I know I joke around, but when it comes down to God, I don't mess around with Him!" Lindy spoke honestly and sincerely to her friend.

"You stood up before God and told all those people that you would take care of that man, and forsake all others for him. All I'm saying is, Alisha, that's your *husband*. I've been around y'all for a long time, and I've see that man go from nothing to something—and share all of that with *you*. He helped you with school and your career; and all

I'm saying is, if he did all of that, *don't* leave him while he's down."

"I just don't know what to do...I feel so confused right now," Alisha confessed. "There's a part of me that wants to move on because it seems like the sky's the limit in this new situation; but when I think about Darien, I do think about everything he's done for me. I think about how he sacrificed for me—and I do feel bad that we're not together during this trying time for him; but I just feel so confused and conflicted within myself...I really don't know what to do."

"I know I probably should catch on fire for even telling you this; but maybe you should pray," Lindy said. "Go to church tomorrow and talk to Pastor Jones—maybe he'll help you."

"Yeah, maybe you're right," Alisha sighed, "maybe I should go to church tomorrow; but in all honesty, I feel so guilty. I feel like as soon as I walk in the door everybody is just going to start looking at me, like they already know what I did—and then I will feel all nasty in church."

"How can you have been a church girl all of your life, and not understand the number one principle about church?," Lindy asked, exasperated. "The number one thing is *forgiveness*. Without that, there would be no church and without that, none of us would even be here. I don't even go to church, and I know that."

"I know," Alisha said sadly, "but I just don't want a lot of people looking at me."

"That's one of the reasons why I don't even go to church, because churches become a place where everybody is focused on everybody else—and not God," Lindy said disgustedly. "But church can't be about people. It must be about God."

"Well come on, let's go together," Alisha suggested. "I need you to be with me...I'm really weak."

"I'll go with you, but you have to wake me up in the morning," Lindy told her. "I haven't seen Pastor Jones in so long, he'll probably put me out of that church as soon as he sees me."

"You're probably right," Alisha laughed, "but it's been a little while since I went myself. But Lindy, getting back to what you said—think about this whole thing. It almost seems impossible to get me and Darien back on speaking terms; I'm just so overwhelmed with this whole situation."

"I hate to sound like one of those old church mothers, but pray about it," Lindy said. She got up, yawning. "I'm getting ready to go to bed, because the only way that I'm going to church is if I go to sleep right now. If I stay up any longer, you'll be in church solo."

Lindy's phone began to ring, and she rushed to the back to answer it in her bedroom. Alisha stayed in the living room on the couch with her pillow and a blanket, and watched TV. She thought about the words that Lindy had spoken to her as she drifted off to sleep.

On Sunday morning at 11:45, Lindy, and Alisha walked into the church and sat on the back pew and saw Pastor

Jones make his entrance into the sanctuary as the choir was singing. Moments later, Pastor Jones stood at the podium and delivered a sermon about regaining territory that the enemy stole. Listening to Pastor Jones tell of intimate encounters he'd had in his life and how God allowed him to regain those things he'd lost hit home for Alisha. She came down to the front of the church with tear-stained eyes; she stood there, along with a few other people out of the congregation, for special prayer. Pastor Jones had said one significant thing that continued to stand out in Alisha's mind even after leaving the altar: she could still hear him say, "It's not too late to get back what you lost."

After the church service, Pastor Jones stood at the door of the church, and shook hands with all of his congregants as they left. Alisha walked past, and said what was on her heart.

"Pastor, you really touched me today," she said.
Pastor Jones smiled at Alisha and hugged her.

"To God be the glory for the things He has done," he said.

"Definitely! I give glory to God; everything you said is exactly what I needed to hear."

"My prayer for you, my child, is that you take what you heard and apply it to your life." He hugged her again.

"I'll be praying for you," he said.

As Alisha and Lindy walked down the stairs of the church, Alisha got a phone call from Deana; Alisha looked at her phone and decided not to answer.

"You should've answered it and broken it off with her, and told her you're going back to your husband," Lindy said candidly. "I don't mean to sound all spiritual and I'm not really big on prophecy, but Alisha, *everything* that he said in today's sermon was tailor-made and custom fit for you! Forget about all that stuff that you've been entangled with, all the stuff that you've been going through—and do just like Pastor Jones said: start over again, and regain your territory."

On the ride home from church Lindy told Alisha, "I am so hungry...I'll tell you what—I want some black eye peas, corn bread, turnip greens, and some pork chops—then after that, I can lay down for a little while...so as soon as we get home, I want you to go and get started on it." Alisha looked at Lindy as though she'd lost her mind.

"Get started on it?! Girl, I'm *not* cooking all of that stuff," she declared.

Lindy just smiled at Alisha. "Consider it rent," she said.

"Yeah, right," Alisha said good-naturedly.

They arrived at Lindy's apartment.

"Talking about all of that food has me hungry now," Alisha said. "Now I'm in the mood to cook."

They went on into Lindy's apartment, and Alisha went to the bathroom to change clothes. Walking into the kitchen, Alisha heard a song on the radio that the choir sang earlier in church. She went into the refrigerator and pulled out the fixings for Sunday dinner. While Alisha prepared the food, Lindy got a phone call as she was on the way back to her bedroom.

"Who was that?," Alisha hollered down the hallway, being nosy.

"Stay out of my personal life," Lindy hollered back.

"I *am* your personal life," Alisha joked. "You know, nobody likes you but me—I'm all you've got."

The afternoon went by slowly, and as the food was cooking, Alisha went into the living room and turned on the football game. She realized she'd done it out of habit, from being with Darien; she wasn't really paying attention to the TV, and grabbed a magazine to look through. All of a sudden, there was a knock at the door.

"Could you go ahead and get that?," Lindy yelled to Alisha from the bedroom.

Alisha went to open the door, and found herself face to face with Darien. For a moment, they both stood there awkwardly, staring at each other, until Darien said "hi".

"How you are doing?," Alisha asked, still shocked to see him.

"Fine," he answered, walking in and closing the door behind him. As he looked toward the living room, his eyes went right to the TV.

"What's the score?," he asked.

"I don't know...I just turned it on, I wasn't really watching it."

They just stood there; Alisha was at a loss for what to say or to do.

"Can I sit down?," Darien finally asked. Thankfully, Lindy walked up and took control of the situation.

"Of course you can," Lindy said, "come on and go to the table with us, I think the food is done."

"Uh, yes...the food is done," Alisha repeated, finally finding her voice.

Darien's attention was grabbed by the football game. Darien turned from a commercial and stood in front of the TV, channel surfing for another game.

"That's typical," Lindy chuckled, shaking her head.

"Give me a minute, I'm coming in there," Darien said, still flipping through channels.

"Lindy, can I talk to you in the back for a second?," Alisha said quietly.

She grabbed Lindy by the hand, pulled her into the bathroom, and closed the door.

"Lindy, why did you do this?!," she whispered furiously, "why didn't you tell me that Darien was coming over here?"

"If I would've told you, you probably wouldn't have cooperated," Lindy stated calmly. "I normally don't try to get into your business; but you two need each other. Tell the truth—you all are miserable without each other," she said.

The sad, empty look on Alisha's face confirmed what Lindy had just said. She continued to speak.

"You know those phone calls that I've been getting all day and all night? Well the truth is, that was Darien calling me—and I've been trying to coach him through this, too," Lindy confessed, "so the only way I can resolve this is to bring you two together for you to try and find some common ground to work things out."

"He doesn't want to work anything out with me," Alisha said bitterly.

"Alisha, you have to drop this attitude," Lindy insisted. "Remember that you violated *him* just like you violated you, so don't go sit at the table like you're the victim. Go on and get your husband back—and get your life back."

Lindy walked out of the bathroom and into the kitchen where Darien was sitting at the table, texting. She sat down.

"Get to work, Hazel," she told Alisha jokingly.

"Whatever!," Alisha smirked.

There was a knock at the door. Lindy stood up and smiled; "that's my cue," she said, heading for the door.

"That's your cue for what?," Alisha asked, a confused look on her face.

"That's my date," Lindy said, "and this dinner is one of those dinners for *two*, because I'm leaving—I'll be back later. Be good, you two."

Lindy opened the door and smiled up at the gentleman standing there; "give me one second, I'll be out in a minute," she told him. She turned back to Alisha, giving her a knowing look.

"I know you all, so I'll be back late," she said. "Change the sheets when you get through—and don't do nothing nasty on my couch."

Darien looked up from his phone, feeling put on the spot.

"That's not going to happen," he sputtered.

"You never know," Lindy winked, closing the door behind herself.

Silence filled the kitchen as Alisha set Darien's plate on the table. She sat down and they both began to eat. Alisha's phone vibrated with a text message from Lindy:

Don't sit there in silence—talk to the man, Alisha!

She replied to Lindy's text message with *LOL*.

She had a smile on her face.

"What's that all about?," Darien asked.

"It's Lindy," she laughed, "she knows me like a book." Darien just smiled self-consciously, holding his head down and returning his attention to his dinner again. As he finished the last portion of his meal, he turned to Alisha.

"This was really good," he complimented her.

"Thank you. I did the best that I could do with what I had," she replied.

Alisha got up from the table, took the plates to the sink, and began washing the dishes; she was grateful to have something to do to keep busy.

"You can go in the other room and watch football," she suggested.

"No, I'd rather stay," Darien said. "Alisha, I want to talk to you."

He got up to take a closer seat beside Alisha as she washed the dishes and put the food away.

"I can help you," he offered.

"That's alright, I've got it…just talk to me," Alisha said.

"Alisha," Darien said, taking a deep breath, "this is really difficult for me to say. But in spite of all that we've been through together—even that whole situation with Deana—you're still my wife, and I love you...and I know that there are certain things that I've done to leave you open so that somebody else could come in," he said, "and I'm sorry for not being the man that I could've been for you. I know I don't have the means right now to live the life style that we once lived, but baby...I want you to come home with me. Crazy as this may sound, Lindy actually does make sense in the time of trouble."

Alisha smiled and turned around from the sink; she looked at Darien.

"You know, I was thinking that same thing," she said.

"The things that she said to me...I even had to stop and just look at the phone, because I was blown away at who was telling me all of this good advice," Darien said, amazed.

"Yeah, she does have that effect," Alisha agreed.

"She will shock you one way or the other; there's one thing that she brought to my attention. Alisha, she reminded me that we made vows to God—that's for better or for worse. So even at our lowest of times, I'm willing to love you unconditionally," Darien said.

He stood up behind Alisha.

"I'm not really with all of this emotional stuff, but one thing I can say is I would rather be on my death bed with you, than to be in my best days without you. You're the best thing in my life, Alisha. I remember, as a kid, being in church one Sunday with my mom; and the preacher said that a man should love his wife like Christ loved the church. Just recently I found out what he was talking about," Darien continued. "I'm supposed to sacrifice my selfish, independent ways, for the good of our relationship. Now I understand that more than ever in my life, and I'm willing to do that. I can say that this is not going to be an easy process for me to transition into the husband that God would have me to be; but I need His help and I need your support. That's the only way this will happen. Alisha, I love you...and I'm not willing to go another day without you."

"I feel the same way, Darien," Alisha said, with a tear in her eye. "I was wrong for everything I did; for everything I said to you that was not true, I'm sorry. I promise that I won't hold another secret from you. Everything is out in the open."

Alisha embraced Darien. "I repent to God for what I did to you, and I repent to you; and I'm asking that you forgive me...I'm *so* sorry for what I did."

Alisha began to cry, and Darien embraced and kissed her.

"I love you...and I do forgive you," he said, kissing her passionately. "I want you to come back to me. I don't care about what was done, I just want my heart back."

He kissed her again, then they paused, looking at each other. Alisha began unbuttoning his shirt. She pushed him down in the chair and began to make passionate love to him.

Later that night, around 12:30, Lindy walked through the door to a pitch-black house. She turned on the lamp and looked at the couch, noticing that Alisha was not there. *They must be in the bedroom,* she thought, *but I didn't see Darien's truck outside.* She walked back to the bedroom and saw that her bed had been untouched; she immediately sent Alisha a text message: *are you okay?* A few minutes passed, but there was no response. Lindy changed clothes, and right before bed she went into the kitchen. She smiled to herself; there was a note on the refrigerator that said, "It worked!"

Chapter 8

Now it's just us

Three days later, Alisha was on the couch at home, doing the last section of her homework, when she received a text message from Deana.

Long time no hear from, stranger, the text said.

I've just been busy, but do you have time today? I need to talk to you, Alisha answered.

What about? We can talk right now.

I'd rather talk to you in person, it's important.

I'll pick you up in about two hours for lunch. Where are you?

I have a few errands I have to run, so as soon as I get through I'll call, and you just tell me where to meet you, Alisha texted.

Okay, Deana agreed.

Alisha finished her homework and started her day running errands. Two hours later, Alisha was sitting across the table from Deana. The waitress came up to the table.

"Can I start you two off with something to drink?," she asked.

"Iced tea with a side of lemon," Deana ordered.

The waitress looked at Alisha. "And for you?," she asked.

"Just water," Alisha said evenly.

Deana looked at her. "Why are you looking like that?," she demanded. "What's wrong?"

Alisha sighed. "Honestly, there's a lot going on."

"Tell me what you wanted to talk to me about," Deana said.

"I don't think I can do this anymore...I don't feel like I can go on like this," Alisha said simply. "I disrespected my covenant with God, I've lied to my husband and crossed the line that I said I would never cross...I just simply can't do this. It's not right."

As she was speaking, the waitress came back to the table with their drink orders.

"Are you ladies ready to order?," she asked pleasantly.

"No...I don't think we'll be eating," Deana said flatly.

"Okay, just signal for me if you change your mind," the waitress said, stepping away from the table.

Deana turned to Alisha, hurt and disappointment in her voice. "Alisha! What about all we've been through together?," she demanded. "What about all the things we shared? I gave you everything."

"So now you're throwing that up in my face? Well, I didn't beg you!"

"And neither did you stop me," Deana replied, "you sat back and enjoyed the ride at my expense...you used me!"

"I didn't use you! I gave you something that is priceless to me—and I will never get it back."

"And what's that?," Deana sneered.

"Myself! I gave in to something I know isn't right; and now my whole life is changed because of it."

"So what now, Alisha? You break up with me and go back to your husband like I'm nothing—and treat me like the flu, and you're over it now."

Deana grew angrier as she spoke. "Well, it's not going to be that easy for me, I put too much into you to just walk away. I've been there for you when nobody else was there for you, Alisha. So can you honestly sit there and tell me that you have *no* feelings for me, and you really want to let this go?"

"All I'm saying is this is just not right," Alisha said calmly. "I care about you...but maybe we should just be friends."

"Friends, Alisha? Friends?! I'm more than that to you, and you know it!," Deana snapped. "I can't believe you'd try to play me with that 'Let's be friends' crap. Alisha, I know you, I know exactly how you think—I'm not your husband. You can't tell me anything and expect me to fall for it," she said bitterly. "So all of this stuff you're telling me now, and you're trying to look sad, and you're trying to break things off with me—it means nothing to me! Alisha, I love you, and I'm not going to let you walk out of my life! You said you love me, and now it's time for you to keep your end of the bargain...remember when we were in Atlanta? You said you would never leave me, you wouldn't do me like everybody else—that you will always be there for me...so now it's your turn to keep your end of the bargain."

Now it was Alisha's turn to be angry; she narrowed her eyes as she looked at Deana.

"So what, now you're just going to *force* me to be in a relationship with you?," she said hotly, "I told you I'm in love with my husband, and that's all that matters to me now...my husband comes first."

Deana took her glass of iced tea, and threw it on Alisha, getting her blouse soaking wet. Alisha jumped up from her chair and just walked straight out of the restaurant. Seconds later, Deana ran out behind her as Alisha walked away down the street. She quickly got in her car and drove off. Deana stood there, pleading for her not to leave.

"I love you Alisha," she screamed, "don't leave!" But Alisha drove off into the traffic.

Deana went back into the restaurant and paid for her drink, apologizing to the manager. She went and got in her car, and called Alisha repeatedly. There was no answer. Deana then drove by Alisha's beauty shop, but she was not there.

Two days later, Alisha was cooking breakfast for her husband as he got ready for work. Darien noticed that his wife had a strange look on her face.

"What's wrong, Alisha?," he asked.

"Nothing, I'm fine," she replied.

"Baby...I know this is a smaller place than the house we had; we'll eventually get there."

"Darien it's not that...it's nothing, actually, baby—have a good day," she said, not wanting to bring up her confrontation with Deana. "I want you to be focused, and have a good day today. I love you," she said, giving him a kiss.

"I love you too, baby. Hope you have a good day too."
Darien walked out the door, but before he closed it he came back in.

"I almost forgot," he said, "I have tickets to that play that starts tonight. Why don't we go and check it out?. That is, if you don't have any clients."

"Sounds good. What time is the performance?"

"Eight o'clock."

"Sounds good to me, baby—have a good day."
Alisha went about her day, ignoring the constant calls from Deana and focusing on her excitement about going to the play with her husband.
Later on that evening, Alisha and Darien were enjoying the play. Darien looked at Alisha.

"I've got to go to the bathroom," he said, "I'll be back in a minute."
He got up and left quickly, not wanting to miss any more of the show than he had to, while Alisha laughed hysterically at the play. Alisha was startled by a kiss on her cheek. She looked over, and to her utter surprise, it was Deana.

"What are you doing here?," Alisha demanded, "I'm here with my husband, you can't do this!"

She looked over her shoulder frantically to see if he was on his way back. "Please leave!," she told Deana.

"I'll leave," Deana said, "but you've got to come talk to me in the bathroom when he gets back."

"No; like I already told you, I'm with my husband."

"Alisha, I hate to say this, but…if you don't do it, I'm going to re-introduce myself to your husband and tell him *exactly* what's going on with me and you," Deana warned. She got up and went back to her seat. Two minutes later, Darien came back to his seat. He was troubled by the look on Alisha's face.

"Baby are you alright?," he asked. "Your whole mood has changed."

"It's nothing, I just need to go to the bathroom," she said stiffly.

"You sure you're alright?"

"I'm fine, baby," she insisted. "I just need to go to the bathroom." Alisha got up from her seat and headed for the ladies' room.

Twenty minutes later, Darien looked out into the hallway and still did not see her returning from the ladies' room. Concerned, he walked up to the women's restroom and spoke to a lady he saw coming out of the restroom.

"Excuse me, miss," he said, "is there a lady in there, brown-skinned, wearing a black dress and yellow necklace?"

"Yes, but I think she's busy," the woman replied.

Darien paused for a second; but he couldn't ignore his suspicions for long. He pushed open the women's restroom door and rushed in.

"I knew it!," he shouted.

Alisha turned around in disbelief. It was a nightmare; her husband and her lover were finally standing face-to-face.

"Wait, baby I can explain," she stammered.

"That's right, Alisha," Deana said smugly, "explain! Tell him what is really going on."

"Alisha...what is really going on?," Darien asked, his voice filled with hurt. "Why would you do me like this, in public?!"

"Baby, it's not like that!," Alisha said, desperate to explain.

"Oh, now *he's* your baby," Deana said sarcastically, "so I guess I'm not your baby anymore...well, I'm going to tell the truth! Darien, your wife is in love with me, and I'm in love with her." She grabbed Alisha's hand possessively. "*That's* the real truth."

But to Deana's surprise, Alisha pulled her hand away.

"This is my husband, and I love him," Alisha said firmly. "I told you that."

"But Alisha, you just told me you love me," Deana insisted.

"What?! Alisha, what happened to what you told me?," Darien asked.

"Tell him!," Deana shouted. "Alisha, tell him how he doesn't satisfy you like I do. Tell him you're tired of pretending that everything is okay. Tell him how he doesn't support you in the things you try to do, but you do support him in everything *he* does! Tell him you're not his sex slave anymore—tell him you're free to be with me!"

Darien was crushed, listening to Deana's cruel words as Alisha stood there, speechless.

"How could you do me like this, Alisha?"

At that moment, the security guards came into the restroom.

"I guess you're not half the man I am, because I satisfy her better," Deana taunted.

Darien reached for her, but the security guards grabbed him and pulled them apart.

"I just can't take this anymore!," Alisha cried, running from the bathroom and out of the theater. Darien looked at Deana with fury.

"Leave us alone!," he thundered, "you are really delusional! You're _not_ together—she's in love with me. I will kill you if you come around my wife again!"

"We will see," Deana challenged.

Alisha was nowhere in sight. Darien looked around and called her on her cell phone; but time and again, the voicemail picked up.

Desperate to locate his wife, Darien called Lindy.

"Have you seen or heard from Alisha?," he asked.

"No, I haven't," Lindy answered, picking up the anxiety in Darien's voice. "I thought you guys were at the theater."

"We were...but we got into a altercation."

"Is everything all right?," Lindy asked.

"I'd rather not talk about it. I'll just call you back, but let me know if you hear anything from Alisha, okay?"

###

Early the next morning, Alisha got up and went to her salon. She opened the door, changed the sign to "open", and turned on some gospel music. *I really need to hear something uplifting right now,* she said to herself.

Alisha lifted her head towards heaven.

"God, I really need to hear something from you right now…I don't know what to do," she said aloud, telling her troubles to the Lord. "I feel like I'm so wrong that I can't be right! I love my husband. I really do. God, it feels like I've messed up so bad that I can't come back to You or him…what do I do?"

Suddenly, Alisha heard a sound in the back of the shop near the storage room; she went to see what it was, but saw nothing unusual. When she came back to the front of the salon, who but Ms. Maxwell from the church came to the door.

"Hi, Sweetie Pie!," she greeted Alisha. "Such a beautiful day outside; I came to see if you could do something to an old woman's hair."

"It's good to see you, Ms. Maxwell," Alisha said. "How did you get way across town, and how did you know where my shop was?"

"You can't keep a secret from an old lady, I've got my ways of finding things out," she smiled, then grew serious. "What's wrong, Sweetie? You look troubled."

"It's nothing—nothing you should concern yourself about," Alisha said. "You probably haven't been through some of things I've been through."

"Sweetie Pie, you would be amazed at some of the things that I've been through," Ms. Maxwell said as she went to the styling chair and sat down. "Tell me, what's the problem?"

"I really don't know how to tell you this..."

"Where's your husband?," Ms. Maxwell asked.

"He's at work," Alisha replied.

"No...*where is your husband*?," she repeated.

Alisha began to cry. Ms. Maxwell placed her comforting hand on Alisha's back. "It's okay. I've been where you are before."

"I've just made so many bad decisions and mistakes and I've messed up," Alisha said, opening up to her. "I feel like I can't repair it...the things that I said I wouldn't ever do any more, I find myself doing; and then the things that I know I *should* be doing to preserve and keep my marriage, I'm not even doing! I just feel so lost. I feel like I'm in the middle of nowhere. I'm in another relationship that I thought was something I wanted, but it's really not—but now I don't want to hurt the other person involved, neither do I want to stay in the situation."

"Sweetie Pie, you're not the only person that's' made bad decisions," Ms. Maxwell said gently. "Looking back over my life, I can honestly say I made some very bad decisions. But through it all, I can honestly say God has been faithful."

"Ms. Maxwell, you know I was raised in the church all my life, and I believe in God...but sometimes Ms. Maxwell,

I don't understand why He allows us to go through some of the things that we go through."

"I know you can't see this right now, Alisha, but this will eventually work for your good."

Alisha sighed impatiently. "Ms. Maxwell, I have been hearing that all of my life: that all the bad is going to work for the good, but it seems like it never does," she said sadly. "My husband and I are only a step away from divorce court. We've almost lost everything, and it's just so hard for me to see this working out for my good. We had a fight," Alisha continued. "The other night, I was out with my husband and without my knowledge to me, the other person was following us—and even confronted him. I know how deeply I've damaged him...I saw something different in his eyes that I've never seen before."

"What are you going to do?," Ms. Maxwell challenged her. "Are you going to allow this situation to take your marriage, and take everything from you?"

"What do I do?," Alisha asked helplessly.

"Number one, you have to reprioritize—you've got to start making time for God," Ms. Maxwell said with certainty. "God has to be the center and the focus of your relationship. Then, the next thing you need to do is let go of everything that's not like God; then sometimes you can do better with less. Don't let someone give you the world, just to take you to hell with him; so you actually start to believe 'self' is more important."

"I just never really thought about it like that," Alisha said. "You're right—the more that I received from that person, the more my mind strayed from my reality."

"Well, it's not too late for you to get your husband back," Ms. Maxwell said, "put God first. If you're ever going to get things right, you've got to put things in the right order. First off, have you told God you're sorry?," she asked.

"No, I haven't," Alisha admitted. "I just feel so disconnected from Him...I just don't know how to get back to Him."

Ms. Maxwell took Alisha's hand and said, "let's pray together right now. Just repeat these words after me:

"Father God, I am coming to you as humbly as I know how. I have sinned against you; I have sinned against my covenant with you and my husband. I forgive all trespasses that were done against me. As you forgive all trespasses that I have done against you, I believe, by the power of God, that all my faults and failures are in my past. I am who you say I am, I will do your will. I am no longer halted in between opinions, Lord Jesus, you are the Savior of my life. Satan! I renounce your works; I see your distractions. By the authority of Jesus Christ, this prayer is your eviction notice out of my marriage and out of my life. All of your entry points are closed, and your every assignment is canceled. I am a kingdom woman of God. Now Lord, strengthen my husband, he needs you like never before. Be with him; touch his heart and touch

mine...restore the joy that we once had in our marriage, and we will forever put you first. In Jesus' name, Amen!"

Ms. Maxwell clapped her hands and praised God. She wrapped her arms around Alisha; as Alisha embraced her with tear-stained eyes, she heard a sniffle. She turned around to find Lindy standing there behind them.

"That was so powerful," Lindy said. "Y'all almost made me catch the Holy Ghost." She went over and hugged Alisha, too.

###

About an hour later, Alisha finished Ms. Maxwell's hair.

"When you get through, do something to my hair right quick; I have an appointment I need to make today," Lindy said.

"Lindy, you *must* have an appointment, because I've never seen you up this time of morning," Alisha teased.

"Well, you could say I'm turning over new leaf."

"This must be a new *tree* you're turning over."

"You'll see soon enough," Lindy said.

As Alisha began to take more clients in for the day, she paused to call Darien on his cell phone, but there was no answer. Later on that night, she met Darien at a park they used to go to when they were dating. As she parked her car, she saw Darien sitting on the top of a picnic table. She walked up to him and embraced him, but he didn't return her embrace. When she leaned in to kiss him he turned his head, and her kiss landed on his cheek. He was in no mood for affection from her.

"You played me like a fool," he said simply. Alisha could hear the hurt and disappointment in his voice.

"I'm sorry, Darien...I just don't know how to tell you the depth of how sorry I am, but trust me when I tell you I am so sorry. I love you..."

Darien stopped her in mid-sentence.

"I don't want to hear anything about love, Alisha; for the embarrassment that you caused me, love cannot repair it."

"I know we have issues...but we can work past this."

"Work past this – that's what you want to do, you want to work past this?!," Darien scoffed. "You must be out of your mind to think that we can work past something like this. Your lover confronted me about you—and you told her intimate details about our relationship. And the only thing that *you* can think to tell *me* is you want to work past it! I know I haven't been the best of husbands, but there's one thing for sure—I've *never* let anybody else in on our relationship. Alisha, this just can't be repaired."

"Darien, I love you," Alisha pleaded. "We've been through a lot, I know...but we are still in the beginning stages of our marriage. We can still save this; we just need to put God first."

"How come you didn't think about putting God first when you were lying to me—and then in the bed with another woman?," he asked coldly.

He was right; Alisha had to accept the truth of what he said to her.

"I'm sorry," she said, "I'm truly, truly sorry, Darien. She was giving me attention that you were just not giving me at the time, and I just got caught up in some of the things she did. Some of things she said just made me feel a certain way...and I just was overwhelmed with it."

"Well that makes two of us, 'cause I'm overwhelmed too, Alisha. I want a divorce!"

Alisha broke down in tears. Darien walked off and left her behind; with tears in his eyes, he got into his truck and drove away. Alisha watched him leave, saying to herself, *I know it's over for sure now.* Slowly, she got up, got in her car, and drove away too. She drove to a bar, went inside, and seated herself at the bar.

"Just give me something...I don't care what it is," Alisha told the bartender.

"What's wrong?," he asked, looking at her strangely.

"My husband left me," she said sadly.

The bartender looked at her with sympathy; it was his job to make his customers feel better, not worse, so he tried to be upbeat.

"Maybe it's time to start over," he said. He walked away and came back with a fancy-looking drink. "Here," he said, "don't worry, everything be all right. All your drinks are on me."

A lady standing next to Alisha turned around to her and spoke.

"Don't listen to him," she said, "stay with your husband...stay even if it gets difficult. I know it gets hard sometimes—there's a lot of ups and downs—but stay with your husband."

Alisha shook her head sadly, sipping on the drink. "You don't even know the half of it," she whispered.

Then the lady showed Alisha her wedding ring.

"Many times I've taken this ring off, and said I was done," she said to Alisha. "I probably can't even count how many times he said he was leaving, packed his clothes, and left. He can't even count the reasons why, 31 years later, we're still together...it's because of commitment."

"What do you do when you've broken your commitment and he walks out, and there's no chance of starting over again?"

The lady looked at her and smiled. "We have the greatest power a woman possesses," she said.

"I don't think sex will do it this time," Alisha said. "He won't even touch me or look at me..."

"I'm not talking about sex," the lady said, pointing up to the sky, "I'm talking about Him. Marriage and relationships are all God's idea, so He's the only one that can fix it."

After a few moments, the woman excused herself. "I'll be right back," she said, and walked off into the crowd of people that were standing around. Alisha turned back around and faced the bar.

"Would you like another one?," the bartender asked.

"No...I'm getting ready to leave," she said. Alisha stared off into space for a moment, and then got up to leave. She left the bar and went back to Lindy's house. Laying on Lindy's couch, she quickly drifted off to sleep.

The sound of the door closing behind someone woke Alisha from her sleep. Alisha grabbed her phone and checked the time; *where is she going so early on a Sunday morning?*, she wondered. She just laid there for moment, then got up and looked again at the time. *I am too late for church*, she said to herself. She turned on the TV; *I'll just watch it from home.*

With the first channel she turned on, the minister's message went straight to her heart:

"Stop making excuses, get up and do what God called you to do! It's not too late. Your blessing is waiting on you, but you've got to get up and move."

After hearing that statement from the minister on TV, Alisha got up and had a burst of energy; she made up her mind to go to church.

###

When Alisha walked through the doors of the church, Pastor Jones was doing altar call.

"There might be somebody in this congregation who feels like they're at the end of their rope...you've tried all you can try, you've done all you can do. You gave your best—now let Jesus do the rest! Come down to this altar right now; I want to pray for you..."

Silly Women & Sleepy Men

Before she could even find a seat, Alisha found herself heading towards the altar. She immediately walked down to the altar to join the others that were already there. Pastor Jones asked for all those who came to the altar for prayer to bow their heads and close their eyes; he then began to pray. Alisha stood there crying, releasing her burden. At the close of his prayer, the pastor asked everyone to hug one another and say, "it's going to be okay." Alisha hugged a few people and started to walk right back out of the church; she opened the door to leave...and then she saw Darien, walking up closer to her. She opened her mouth to speak, but no words would come.

"Don't talk, just listen," Darien said to her. "Alisha, I need you, I'm not whole without you...I feel like I can't even breathe without you. Alisha, something happened to me last night that I can't explain; I heard a voice last night, and I wasn't asleep, I wasn't drinking—and nobody was in the room with me."

He continued, looking Alisha in the eyes. "The voice said to me, 'it's not too late. Stop making excuses', so Alisha, I came here today to tell you that I want to start over. I do love you; I'm only half a man without you. I promise to give you the attention that you need from me. I promise you that I will work my fingers to the bone to make sure you have all the things that you want and need...but I won't work so hard that I neglect you and leave you alone, because I understand that you need me—but I want you to understand that I need you even more. Alisha, I want to know God, I want to know Him in the way that you know Him. Last night after my dream, Alisha, I got down on my knees and told God two things. First, I told Him I was sorry, because I didn't know how good He was to me until I lost everything. The second thing I told God is that if He never gave me back any of the material things I once had, that I wanted a new start with you, so I'm making the first step...Alisha, I love you, let's start over."

Alisha was overjoyed.

"Only if you promise me one thing," she said, with tears flowing down her face, "that we will always put God first—and I promise you I will always be honest with you. I'm sorry for the hurt and pain that I caused you."

"Everything is okay," Darien said. "I wasn't there for you like a man should be."

He held her tight and kissed her passionately.

"I do", all over again," Alisha said.

"Good...because we will tonight, all over again," Darien said, kissing her again.

Alisha's phone began ringing in her purse, which hung on her shoulder.

"Excuse me," a woman's voice said; Alisha felt a light bump, and her purse slid from her shoulder. The woman who'd bumped her reached down to grab Alisha's purse.

"I'm so sorry," she said, and when the woman looked up, Alisha realized it was the same lady from the bar. Alisha stood there in amazement.

"Commitment," the lady said, giving Alisha a knowing smile as she proceeded to walk away.

"Wait a minute," Alisha called after her, "I need to get your name."

The lady turned back around and said, "my name is Grace."

"Who is that, somebody you know?," Darien asked.

"It's a long story," she said, still in amazement.

Her phone started ringing again; "it must be Lindy," she said. She scrounged around in her purse trying to find the phone. She pulled the phone out and looked at the caller ID, and to her surprise, it was Deana. She looked at Darien and showed him the caller ID.

"Baby this is not the life that I want to live anymore. I want to be the woman that God called for you."

"I believe you. I trust you."

"I am changing my number Monday morning," she said. Darien held her close in his arms.

Epilogue

A little less than a year later, Lindy went to see Alisha in the hospital. Walking down the hospital halls, Lindy began to count doors nervously... "503, 504, 505...this is the room," she said. "Knock, Knock," she called out as she pushed the door open and walked into the room with Anthony.

"Hi," Darien said, as he sat up in the chair, stretched his arms, and yawned. "You two must have called each other on the elevator on the way up," he said.

Anthony looked at Lindy and smirked. Lindy smiled back at him.

"No, we came together," she said. "Where is Alisha?"

"Alisha is gone with the doctor," Darien said, "but back to you two: so, you're a couple, and nobody even told me...Anthony, that's just wrong, man—you know you could've told me," he said jokingly. "You're in for it now, you know. Lindy snores extremely loud."

"Stop, Darien," Lindy said. She playfully pushed Anthony as he laughed with Darien. "You *definitely* better stop," she told Darien.

"When you and Alisha were dating, I never said anything to her about the 'hammer time' that goes on in your shoes," she cracked. "Your feet are so hard and crusty, they tear up the carpet when you walk barefoot!"

The door opened, and Alisha came back with the doctor and the baby. When the little 8 pound and 5 ounce bundle of joy came into the room, everything else stopped. Everyone watched her as she lay asleep.

"She looks like an angel," Lindy said softly.

"Now that's the one thing we can agree on," Darien said.

"I can't wait to pick her up," Lindy added.

"She's beautiful, man—congratulations," Anthony said to Darien.

Lindy went over and hugged Alisha. "I'm so proud of you," she told her friend. "I want to do anything and everything to help you with this baby...what is her name?"

"Maya," Alisha said proudly.

"Why did you name her that?," Lindy asked, "I thought you were going to name her something else."

"You have to be careful what you name your children," Alisha replied. "I started looking at that, and the meanings of certain names, and I changed my mind."

"Plus, I like that that name better anyway," Darien added.

"Yes, she is a little angel," Dr. West agreed. As Dr. West was speaking, a nurse came in and handed him a folder. He opened the folder and paused for a second.

"Alisha, Darien, I want to discuss some of the things that we ran tests on...but it might be best that I discuss it with just you two," Dr. West said.

Instantly, Darien became worried. "What's wrong?," he asked. He stood up out of the chair and confronted the doctor.

"What's wrong?!," he demanded.

"I think it's best that you relax," Dr. West told Darien. "Everything is going to be okay."

"Can you guys excuse us?," Alisha asked.

With a puzzled look on their faces, Anthony and Lindy agreed to wait outside.

"But as soon as the doctor is through, I'm coming back," Lindy said, "I'm just going outside for minute."

After Lindy and Anthony had left the room, Dr. West turned to Alisha and Darien. "We ran tests on little Maya and we found the trait for sickle cell anemia," he said. This is a trait that is transferred from the parent to the child. That's why we asked you earlier to give blood samples from both of you, to trace where this came from. This disorder is hereditary," Dr. West explained, "it comes from a parent or runs down a family line. Alisha, has any of your family ever had sickle cell?"

"No! No one that I know of in my family ever had anything like that," she said.

When Dr. West began to talk about treatment methods, Alisha noticed that he said nothing to Darien. Alisha turned to Dr. West.

"Is it a possibility that she got it from her father?," she asked.

"Yes," Dr. West responded, somewhat uncomfortably.

"I'm confused," Darien said. "You say it is possibly hereditary; but I've never had anything like that in my family."

Dr. West looked at them directly as he spoke. "That's the next part I wanted to talk to you guys about—and that's why I asked your friends to step out," he said. "I hate to be the one to tell you this, but we tested your blood...*Darien, you're not the father."*

Until.....

Stay connected to us through our Social Media

Email us: mailrobertgreen@yahoo.com

www.robertgreenministries.com

Also look out for more titles from Pastor Robert Green

Made in the USA
Charleston, SC
29 August 2014